ABOUT THAT PREGNANCY GLOW

TWYLA RIGHTER

About That Pregnancy Glow
Twyla Righter

Paperback Edition
Copyright © 2018 (as revised) by Twyla Righter

City Lights Press
An Imprint of Wolfpack Publishing
6032 Wheat Penny Avenue
Las Vegas, NV 89122

This book is a work of fiction. Any references to historical events, real people or real places are used fictitiously. Other names, characters, places and events are products of the author's imagination, and any resemblance to actual events, places or persons, living or dead, is entirely coincidental.

All rights reserved. No part of this book may be reproduced by any means without the prior written consent of the publisher, other than brief quotes for reviews.

ISBN: 978-1-64119-255-2

ABOUT THAT PREGNANCY GLOW

INTRODUCTION

I'm leaning over the sink, but tilted slightly sideways to make room for the huge belly. Shreds of carrot peel line the sink as I run the peeler down the length of the carrots - getting dinner going for the fam.

Two done, four to go.

My toddler son is jumping up and down on his Dad's lap as he watches me. My husband holds the hopping one with one arm while telling me about his day. I'm too distracted. Those peels look disgusting just sticking in the sink. His voice stops, he has gotten quiet.

"What?" I ask, "What were you saying?"

He starts again, but those darn carrot peels are killing me, they are just so nasty. It's too late. The battle is over. I set the carrots down and start heaving into the sink. But, there is that other problem... my bladder.

I lose control of that too.

Right there, in the kitchen, in front of a fully potty trained three-year-old, I make two puddles.

One in the sink - one on the floor.

And what do the men in the house do? Are they shocked?

Nope - this happens all the time.

They are laughing and tossing a towel my way. It's just another day with me and my special pregnancy glow.

WELCOME TO PREGNANCY!

I am hoping if you picked this book up that it's because you are pregnant and could use a little encouragement. If you're one of those, "I've never felt more alive! I love being pregnant!! I feel so sexy!" kind of women, then I hope you are thanking your lucky stars, every single moment, because you really have been blessed. And I think you can enjoy this book as well, because chances are that you will find something in your pregnancy does turn out to be difficult.

Maybe it will be the breastfeeding, or losing the baby weight, or the changes in your marriage. But if you are like me, and found that pregnancy is about as fun as getting stabbed in the eye, with a stick... over and over... every day... for nine months, well then this is the book for you!

I know that there are plenty of pregnancy books

out there - and a few that are pretty funny too. But, I wrote this for the Moms like me, who ***really*** struggled with pregnancy. I found that during my pregnancies I was desperate for some "misery loves company" camaraderie.

Now, chances are good that your struggles will be different than mine, but I think it's enough just to know there is someone out there who was miserable too. Because, I really do believe that knowing others have gone through the same thing and suffered through it just like you did, helps.

It's just nice to know that you're not the only miserable soul on the planet, and that even for those of us who found pregnancy (and that first year of motherhood) to be difficult, it wasn't impossible. Motherhood is worth all of these miserable moments. It really is. I promise - totally worth all of it.

HOW IT ALL BEGINS

It's different for each of us. For you, pregnancy may have involved work and planning. I was from the other variety. When I found out I had become a mother, I was trying NOT to get pregnant. Regardless of the camp you fall into, we all got here in the same way: Sex.

It's funny how when you are engaging in that particular activity nothing maternal is figuring into it - at all.

I'm certain that whatever I did when I created my first child was pleasantly fun - but I will always resent sex for being fun for men. Isn't it just a bit obnoxious that the contribution our husbands make to creating a new life is so much fun for them? How is sex at all fair? That is ALL that men contribute to the process? Have an orgasm? Seriously?

I have to go through nine of the all-time worst

months of my entire life - and then the childbirth - and then the breastfeeding. His body's contribution? Sex. I kind of hate men for this.

As a religious person, I always assumed the whole "Garden of Eden" story was more of an analogy - or parable. Not meant to be taken literally, but as an explanation of the Pandora's box that evil set upon this world. After pregnancy I am convinced that the story was literal.

THE WHOLE THING.

Eve pissed God off to no end and he cursed women. I have no other way of explaining the complete disparity of fairness in the deviation of fatherly and motherly duties with regard to our bodies. If you ever go to look for justice - don't look at natural order, because there is no way around it - from PMS to Menopause the female is given the shaft!

(Hahaha!! Did you get that??)

Now, back to the "act" of making children -

I have to say...sex - I mean...it's weird - right? Really, it's one of the weirdest things that we ever do. Of course it's fun/weird - but still, weird.

If you don't think it's weird; have your 7 year old kid almost barge in on you - in that second when you are yelling and wondering why the door isn't locked - imagine what you would have said to him to explain what he would have seen.

Just try it:

"Mommy and Daddy were just...."

You sound like an idiot don't you?

Have you used the word 'mature' yet, or 'hormones' or 'puberty'? What about 'feelings'? That word cannot come out of anyone's mouth without making them sound like a jack-ass.

My point is that it's weird. That's all.

Somehow, perfectly normal people who have thoughts and opinions, who vacuum their cars and floss their teeth are suddenly panting, screaming, wet, messy, idiots who are totally oblivious to the world around them. It's a jiggly, floppy, bouncysmellycrazychaos and when it's all finished you do that hobble to the bathroom where you clean up and pull yourself back together - ready to re-enter the world of the normal people- all the while, all of us knowing, that all of us are doing this crazy, weird, thing... and doing it a lot.

BEGINNINGS

Well, let me be the first to break it to you - the fun-weird thing you did that got you pregnant... is the last fun part of this process. Actually that's not true - for some of you pregnancy will make you feel real and womanly and horny. And that's just awesome for you. (Read that with an eye roll and heavy sarcasm.)

Fortunately for me, that last part did not happen. I say fortunately because, while I was completely uninterested in anything but keeping food down for those magical 9 months - my husband's libido couldn't have been lower. What would be worse than him being pretty turned off by pregnant me, and me being all desperate and horny?? Ugh... awkward! But, like I said, that didn't happen.

It had something to do with the baby in between us if we did try, or the fact that I was just lying there trying not to barf, or my horrible, dimply, jiggly, disgusting, pregnant butt. (He never, ever, admitted it; but I saw it a few times in the mirror and it was shocking.) I have asked him why he was so lacking in libido and he says that the worst part was me needing to pause to spit. (I'll talk about that later.)

Whatever it was, there are 2 1/2 years of our married life together in which we had almost no sex at all - and neither one of us was bummed about it.

TRYING TO CONCEIVE

This was an area that I have to say I have very little experience with - but I will give you my limited experience.

Trying to conceive only occurred once in my life. It was with our second child.

Having already experienced the epic nature of my pregnancies my husband was determined that ours would be an only child. So, I asked my husband if we could have another child and he shot me down. No way that he was going to let that happen.

I was a bit irritated here - if we were not on the same page why was it that he got to win automatically? I mean it makes sense in one way - you can't force someone else to become a parent if they don't want to... but why is it that the 'No' vote wins by default?? And doubly annoying that he wanted to do all that was necessary in order to become a parent again... he just didn't want the inevitable consequences to occur.

So I had a talk with myself. "Self," I said, "How are we going to convince this wonderful father and husband that he should enter into another horrible pregnancy willingly?" The obvious answer was that I could not do such a thing. I was pretty bewildered at my willingness to enter into the horror myself. In fact I was a little incensed. If I was willing to do the suffering, how dare he say that being along for the ride was too difficult?

If I was willing to face that giving our child a sibling was worth absolute torture for 9 months of my life then how dare he complain that he'd have to be around me? Well, the conversation with myself had reached the same dead end that the conversation with my husband had reached... except that in the conversation with myself I acknowledged something awful. I acknowledged that I could easily trick my husband into fathering a child.

(I know, this is a horrible thought! - I didn't mean to have it - but it did pop into my mind.) Of course being a sane and rational woman I would never, ever, trick my best friend in the whole world into doing something against his will.

However...

It did occur to me that there was a similar option.

So I finished up my conversation with myself,

thanked myself for my wisdom, and decided to put our plan into action.

I headed to my beloved husband with a determined confidence and told him what needed to be said: "Love of my life," I stated, (My memory has a sweeter demeanor than my reality) "I respect your feelings on the issue of having another child, and I recognize that I cannot force you to do such a thing against your will. But, if you are determined not to have any more children, then you are going to have to be responsible for birth control from now on. Also, I will be wearing lingerie for the foreseeable future while walking around the house."

I was pregnant two months later.

IT'S NOT THAT EASY

The first month after trying to convince my husband to create new life with me was a kind of fun game. I spent a decent amount of time trying to seduce him - which he was enjoying, and he spent a lot of time carting out condoms and making me mad. However, there were a few "accidents" throughout the month and I was just positive I was going to be pregnant.

Having gotten pregnant the first time when I was trying really hard NOT to get pregnant, it seemed weird that trying to get pregnant would require any effort at all. So as the end of that month approached I was obsessing about my symptoms... my tummy was achy - cramps or implantation?? My breasts were tender... PMS or pregnancy?? All of it was just killing me. And then one afternoon I got my period.

I have had my period a gazzillion times in my life - but I remember this time clearly. I was devastated. I had been so hopeful. There had been several opportunities for us to have gotten pregnant. How on earth had it not occurred? If I wasn't pregnant, why not? Was something wrong?

Really, truly, my heart was broken.

Now, I recognize how insensitive I am in saying this. Here I was, in my late twenties - already having a beautiful child and fully aware that I was probably fertile and that I had time to spare and I had only tried one time - one month, of my entire life, and not getting immediate success I was terrified and devastated.

But, I tell you this to impart how important it is to be compassionate and sensitive to our sisters who are trying. It is hard to clarify just how difficult the process can be, and if I can feel that much pain from one unsuccessful month - imagine your friends who have been trying for a year - or more painful still, those who have lost their babies. For women who have hearts for children this process can cause a lot of pain.

ADOPTION

I have always had a heart for adoption.

One of the very best friends of my entire life was adopted when he was an infant. He has gone on to lead an amazing - beautiful life and there is something huge in realizing that his life would never ever have been a fraction of what it is had his parents not snatched him up and called him their own. I have a spot in my heart that believes that there is a child somewhere who needs a mom and that I could be that mom.

I also think my love of adoption comes from some of my own experience.

My Dad died when I was young and so, for much of my life, I was raised by my step-dad. My mother then died in my twenties. Now, when my kids have a ballet performance, the Grandma and Grandpa that come to watch them have zero blood relation to them. My stepfather and stepmother are my family, they are my kid's grandparents and we love each other. Family can be, and often is created with pregnancies and DNA – but that is not what is foundational to family.

Families are made by love. Period. It is cliché, it is simple, and trite, but it is true. The family you make is forged and bonded in love. So I hope that if you are trying to conceive and finding that your body is not going to carry babies that you will be open to finding another road to motherhood – loving a child is always beautiful.

TIPS FOR TRYING TO CONCEIVE

So, here are my best tips from friends I have, who have gone through this.

#1 Ovulation tests work. If you are trying to get pregnant these really can nail down the timing better than anything else.

#2 Don't do something, lay there. Once you are finished with the "baby dance," stay on your back - for as long as possible.

#3 There is an herb called "Vitex" that has helped several women I know conceive. It seems to extend the fertility window by balancing your hormone levels. It takes a few months to really work, but it's got a good track record.

There! That's all I've got. Unless you're trying to con your husband into making a baby when he's not into it, then I suggest you follow my method. Put him in charge of birth control and get in touch with your saucy side.

FIRST TRIMESTER

So you know you're pregnant.

I found out I was a mother in the most bizarre way. I thought I was broken... you know... down there. (I'm not a crazy person.)

I had decided to take up snowboarding. Well, more accurately, my husband decided I should take up snowboarding. We lived in California, and skiing – (which I had done my whole life as a native of Colorado) - was super-duper uncool. "Super-duper" may not have been very cool either.

So... learning to snowboard had me falling, a lot - and without giving you unnecessary details - I fell on my behind really hard and I was pretty sure something got "broken." I spent a couple of months not too surprised that my lady parts were on the fritz - after all the damage I'd incurred during the trauma. But after having gone way too long without a 'friendly visit from Aunt Flo' I decided I should go visit a lady-parts doctor.

I picked a cheap one. I had just signed up for a new insurance plan with my new job (I had deliberately chosen NOT to get the maternity coverage... wanted to save the $10 per month... seriously.) So I found a random OBGYN and made an appointment. I peed in the cup and headed into the room, dreading the exposure I was about to endure for only the second time in my entire life. That was when the most important news I would ever receive was delivered to me.

I will never forget her- the woman who bore me the most incredible news of my life. She was a medical tech, and she was following the trend (this was early 2000-ish) - of shaving off your eyebrows and then drawing them on with a pencil. She also was doing the lip-liner around the mouth but no lipstick on the inside thing. I am not a visual person and I usually cannot seem to be able to remember visual details very well, but I remember her. She didn't even look up at me. She just threw it out there. Splat. With no enthusiasm. Nothing. "So, it looks like you're pregnant."

That was it. The most important news of my entire life! She was announcing that: From that day forward - I would forever be a mother!!! And she said it with the same tone that she would clarify if I, 'wanted fries with that.' In fact, I know I have been asked to add fries with far more enthusiasm.

To this day I just remember staring at her - thinking - "Who are you?"

This is the person who would share the most important moment - THE MOST IMPORTANT announcement of my entire life! My husband, my mother - my sister - my best friends - none of these people were there.

This day that would forever be the pinnacle moment of my life. My days would forever be defined as my life before motherhood and after - and I was sharing it with... well, who was she? I still remember that overwhelming need. I should know her name - she should matter to me. But she didn't, and I didn't matter to her. I didn't even meet the doctor. I told her that I was going to need to leave and I did.

Tada! I figured that I might be pretty far along. I hadn't had a 'special visit' for several months, so it was possible that I was already heading into my 2nd trimester. I now know how silly that is: that I could have been that far into my pregnancy with zero symptoms. (Ha!) It turns out I was just about 5 weeks when I got the news. Then things got really going.

HELLO TOILET MY NEW FRIEND

Pregnancy was always a time in my life in which I became extremely intimately involved with my toilet. You will never spend more time in a bathroom than during pregnancy. It started with needing to pee. Always.

It just happened. One day I was a normal person, I went pee a few times a day- no big deal. Then, in an instant, everything changed. I had to pee constantly.

I remember the exact moment because we were looking for a refrigerator. We were supposed to be picking out a fridge (not that we were making much of a choice we would be getting the cheapest thing we could find - I think we got one for right around $100.) But I couldn't pay any attention because I needed to pee so badly. So I asked where I might find a bathroom and I headed to their "employee bathroom." I came out and looked at a few more options and then I needed to ask if I could use their bathroom - again. It was so embarrassing, and it wasn't like I 'looked' pregnant, there was no way the salesman wouldn't just assume that I had crazy diarrhea or something.

This constant "peeishness" symptom lasted for several weeks. It was odd, for sure, but it almost seemed cute.

I could already envision my pregnancy. Picture me: glowing skin, adorable maternity top on. Pretty face and hair and the jutting little tummy and once in a while I would run off to pee all embarrassed and cute. Aw... can't you imagine cute pregnant me?

Within a week real pregnant me had run that cute idea over. I came face to face with 'morning sickness.' Nothing is more completely insulting than that name. "Morning Sickness."

MORNING SICKNESS / HYPEREMESIS

We are about to embark upon a rather nasty, disgusting, unpleasant portion of my pregnancy that you may want to skip over. For example, if you are currently nauseated, and the sight of toenail fungus commercials has made you ralph, then reading this section is likely to be too much right now. If you are not currently nauseated, or if you are just a glutton for punishment then we can head on down the rabbit hole...

"Morning-sickness??" Really??

How about we call it, all day long, can't keep anything down, somebody shoot me, I wish I could die sickness? You think I'm being melodramatic?? I truly could not keep anything down in those first weeks. Nothing.

I would swallow something - it wouldn't even

land in my stomach - it just did a U-turn on the way down and came right back up. That's a weird feeling. To feel yourself swallow, and then, as though there was a reject button somewhere in the middle of your esophagus, feel that banana just pop right back up. You almost don't know what to do at that point.

And it lasted all day and all night long. Very quickly I was dropping weight and became extremely dehydrated.

Here's the advice I got: Crackers.

"Try crackers!"

I remember wanting to drop kick every single person who told me about crackers.

"You know, it's a good idea to wake up and just lay there and chew a few crackers before you even get out of bed." That was as effective as attempting to muffle a nuclear warhead with a damp towel.

I tried so many things that first pregnancy. My husband ran to the natural grocers and bought me a million types of ginger. We had candied ginger, ginger capsules, ginger ale and boiled ginger as tea.

Chew the ginger - barf the ginger. Sip ginger tea - barf ginger tea. Ginger, peppermint, soda, crackers, brat diets, lemon, preggo pops, aromatherapy…. Everything.

I got some seasickness bracelets. I wore those things for the full 9 months. Just for in case they were helping. They were basically a rubber band with a little plastic doodad that was supposed to be placed on a "pressure point" to stop the nausea.

I tried it all. If you ever have a friend with intense morning sickness or hyper-emesis, please believe them when they say that it's not working. Because, It's - Not – Working!!!

The theory behind why women get sick is that our bodies are at a very tenuous point in fetal development in the first weeks. The baby is developing all of their major organ systems, and every second of those first weeks it could be deadly for us to expose them to any toxin that could harm that development. In fact, women who vomit during the first trimester are much less likely to miscarry, and women with hyper-emesis actually have the lowest miscarriage rates of all. So, for as sorry as you may feel for yourself right now - it is important to remember that this sickness serves a purpose and is protecting your child.

After I entered the second trimester I could keep food down for 20 minutes or so. However, as it stayed down it seemed to build power. It would then explode out of me. I could have made a show of vomiting for distance. I think 9 feet would be a safe number. Seriously, - I am not crazy. That happened.

Fortunately for me, my husband is a Nurse Anesthetist (Nurse who does the same job as an Anesthesiologist). He got me lots of IV hydration - and lots of drugs (which cost a fortune.) But I spent my whole pregnancy sick, sicker than I have ever been in my entire life. I lost weight for 5 months. I broke blood vessels around my eyes and the back of my throat. How any woman, before modern medicine, ever survived this is beyond me.

It is called "hyper-emesis," and it's very rare. Kate Middleton, the British royal, had it as well. She appears to have been one of the fortunate ones who fully recovered in later trimesters - I was not. I did improve and did get to where I was vomiting far less often - but I never fully stopped vomiting until the moment my babies were born. If you have morning sickness right now, I want to encourage you that I am in a very, very, very, small minority. Less than two percent of women continue vomiting for their entire pregnancies. The odds are that you will start feeling better soon.

There were some things that I did try that did help.

#1 - Quit hoping you won't throw up. You are going to throw up and it's going to be awful, so it is better to start trying to find foods that will stay down longer and 'throw up better.'

#2 - Dairy 'throws up better' than ANYTHING. If you can live on yogurt do it, because it hardly even hurts to throw up yogurt. If you can't live on yogurt (and I couldn't) carry "Tums" around and chew a few up and swallow them right before you vomit. They will save your esophagus and throat from a lot of damage.

#3 – Chewing tums is also going to help save your teeth. You want to have an awkward conversation? Try to convince your dentist that you aren't a bulimic after he's checked out your post- hyper-emesis teeth. Months of vomiting do a lot of damage. A dentist later told me NEVER to brush my teeth after I vomited. Instead he said to swish some baking soda and water around in my mouth. This was great because brushing my teeth made me gag, and I could swish the baking soda without it making me sick.

#4 - Go to the doctor and get some IV hydration. THIS IS THE BEST TRICK!! You will not believe how much this helps with nausea. It doesn't work for all that long, but for a while you really do feel so much better.

#5 - If your doctor blows you off and you are vomiting a few times a day, go and get a new doctor. Some doctors actually believe that morning sickness is just psychological, (or maybe they are just jerks) - but I have heard of women who were treated horribly while they were sick. If you're just really nauseated, but not vomiting, then it makes sense to just leave it alone. But constant vomiting is really damaging to your body and to your heart. There is nothing I have ever experienced that has made me more miserable. Get a doctor who cares.

#6 - Get some drugs… medications. I took Phenergan, which I loved - it knocks you out! And when you're miserable who wouldn't rather just be asleep? If you don't have to work, or have another child to look after then it is amazing.

I also took Zophran and a couple of generic versions of the drug. They really do work. If you're really sick you will swear that it isn't working at all. Until you try to skip a dose - then you will start throwing up non-stop and realize that it was actually helping all along.

But... I also took a drug called Reglan.

I was still in the first trimester with my first child and I was in the middle of non-stop vomiting. I had heard of morning sickness and was doing my best to suffer through it. I was home from work and after several trips to the bathroom that morning started blacking out. I called my husband who was working at the hospital and told him I was afraid I was going to pass out, so he told me to come and get checked out.

I drove to the ER, pulling over to the side of the road whenever I needed to, and managed to pull into the hospital in one piece. He met me and got me checked in and into a hospital bed. They popped an IV in my arm and as I started to get hydrated I started feeling a lot better... and then I started to feel a lot worse. My heart was racing and I was getting stressed out and paranoid. I couldn't figure out what was wrong and since my husband was still working

I was all alone with one of those curtains around me.

I suddenly realized I must be one of those people who has a phobia about hospitals because I was going to freak out if I had to spend another second in there.

I called the nurse and begged her to get my husband and get me checked out. He tried to talk me into waiting and was confused about my urgency as he headed me back to the car. I was incredibly jittery and once we were out of the hospital I started explaining to him that I could never go back, that I couldn't take the hospital and was sure I had a phobia. He started laughing.

Apparently, the drug Reglan makes some people really anxious. I am some people. So if your doctor prescribes Reglan for you, make sure you have your husband or someone with you for that first dose. For most people it's fine, but for a few of us, it's a really unpleasant ride.

7 - Ignore... well, a lot of people.

Ignore the people who wonder if you're sick because you secretly don't really want to be pregnant. Ignore the people who ask if you've tried crackers and soda. Ignore the people who say they were really sick too, but they just refused to throw up. Ignore the people who say that you might feel better if you just took a shower, or took a walk, or cleaned up the house a bit. You too may have said some of that sort of inane crap if you didn't know how you felt.

Ignore them - it will be their turn soon enough, and when they can't figure out why their baby won't stop crying, you can just tell them that your baby cried too, but you just have a really calm energy that soothes your baby... they will love that.

ESCAPISM

Here is my final bit of advice. Get sucked into a series of some kind. Harry Potter got me through two pregnancies. Reading is harder to do sick so if you can find a TV series that might be better. <u>Lost</u> would be a good one. Begin watching something that will last a long time, that you could watch episode after episode and become completely absorbed by. You will find that your ability to distract yourself can help keep the vomiting at bay for longer periods.

It is very hard to distract yourself, I found that if I was watching television I would vomit the second there was a commercial. And while you will not want to go for too long without vomiting (remember, it builds… pressure). Stretching the time between bouts is important, and it is also important for your sanity to escape the misery of your reality as best you can.

If you can find a series and get sucked into it that

will help these difficult weeks pass more quickly. But, it will convince people that you are milking the whole thing too. It is important to check yourself and to be honest if you are sucked into a book and have started to improve, but just can't move until you know if Hermione is going to get caught.

However, if you're still vomiting several times a day, then you just stick your nose right back into that book and get yourself lost in a better world.

UNSOLICITED ADVICE

Here's another thing that happens once you become a mother: people feel way too comfortable giving you their opinion - on everything. I have had people tell me I am too firm with my kids, people tell me what I should or shouldn't eat or drink while pregnant, people lecture me on what is too dangerous for me or my children. It's just an annoying part of motherhood - but my high point for inappropriate comments had to be when a man approached me in the airport. I was a flight attendant and I had to fly during part of my pregnancy. I had just landed, ran to the nearest garbage can and started retching. A "kind soul" decided to come up behind me and let me know he would appreciate it if I would do that in the bathroom. I still wish I could have turned around and finished up all over him.

I know we all do it, we get annoyed with people

around us - but I'll tell you what, it's important to remember that a person could be going through something awful that you don't understand.

I threw up all over myself, and my car on several occasions, which made me cry in self-pity - all the while trying not to crash. I'm certain that people were probably furious with my erratic driving - but life happens. Maybe a driver in front of you is a terrible driver, but maybe she is just trying to find a place to pull over so she can throw up.

I'll bet the man who stopped me in the airport thought that I was hung over and was shaming me. And being sick as a dog from pregnancy was bad enough, but what if it had been from chemo?

I'M AWAKE... NO... NO, I'M NOT.

Tired. That was the other thing about the first trimester. I was so tired. Benadryl tired. All the time.

I would wake up in that crazy, heavy, fog and spend the entire waking time truly excited to get back to sleep. Some of the problem was likely that real life was so miserable - what with the vomiting and all - but the act of sleeping was delicious to me. It called to me with a siren's song.

This did lift however; by the second trimester I lost the intense exhaustion. I think that (along with the vomiting) much of the discomfort of the first trimester is just that your body is doing such important stuff. Keeping that baby safe makes your body determined to keep anything that could be dangerous from coming into your body - and growing a nervous system that will be capable of somersaults, love, and long division requires a lot of energy.

So you vomit, and sleep... and repeat.

WEIRD FOOD CRAVINGS: DID YOU KNOW PICKLES TASTE AMAZING?

Another bizarro part of the "pregnant process" - wanting weird foods. This again seems to be because your body is trying to build a person - so it's not too subtle about what it wants - more or less demands really.

Everyone's cravings are different; I have even known women who had Pica. Have you heard of that one? If you were thinking I might be crazy... these girls would want to lick the dirt off of the side of cars! That's crazy! (It relates to malnutrition of some kind - and let me just say if you find yourself craving dirt or soap or some other weirdness - call your doctor because there is probably something important that you need.)

I know that pickles are kind-of cliché' but that was the thing I would eat. I think it might be because of the vomiting - and the spit. Have I told you about the spit yet? I'll get back to that one.

Oh the pickles - that intense vinegar flavor! It just seemed like the juice of the Gods. I would suck on them. Eat them really slowly (after all I was going to be throwing them up soon enough - making sure they were as mushy as possible was important.) Whenever I could, I would buy myself time by slowly chewing on a pickle. It was a love affair of sorts.

I also remember swallowing a gulp of orange juice and believing I would die if I didn't drink more. It was as though there was nothing in the world but that orange juice. I was so desperate to drink some - but so terrified of throwing that orange juice up! I mean; can you imagine how bad citrus burns when you vomit? Ugh!

I have never had any other craving that was as intense. I would have run through fire.

I was shaking as I held the carton up and took a swallow directly from the carton. I put it in the fridge and walked away. I didn't make it two steps. I turned around and opened the fridge and started chugging. I was terrified! I couldn't stand the thought of throwing up that orange juice, but I couldn't not drink it - I was beyond compelled.

There were other insane cravings - a burger, a bagel, and a burrito. Meals that I will never forget how desperately I wanted - meals that I will never forget how awful it was to purge.

The other weird thing about nausea was the stuff that would trigger it. Commercials for foods that sounded disgusting would throw me over the edge. Toothpaste commercials, toilet cleaners, comments about feet – and anything involving the mouth really. Ugh!

The worst was the smell of the laundry soap isle in the grocery store! I hated that isle.

Although all smells were bad. The smell of hot asphalt, the smell of food, …. the smell of my husband.

Yeah, that was pretty sucky for him. I didn't sleep with him most of the time when I was pregnant.

He normally smells wonderful to me. He wears really good deodorant, but doesn't wear a bunch of cologne - so I love cuddling up to him and smelling him. But man alive, when I am pregnant he stinks so bad I can't take it.

I eventually realized that a big factor was the soap he was using. I don't remember what brand it was, just a normal grocery store cheap brand. But it was killing me. Somewhere into my last pregnancy I realized that the natural grocer stores didn't make me sick and had him switch to an all-natural soap and it helped a ton. The natural soap also helped me to shower more too.

The worst smell ever was the smell of water. I could not drink water, couldn't smell water, or ice. I could always smell whatever had been in a freezer with the ice - if there was some smoked sausage in the freezer I was fully aware when I got a whiff of that ice.

I couldn't handle transitional smells. So if I was going to get into a car - the act of leaving the outdoors and entering the car would make me throw up. I would cover my nose with a shirt or jacket and breathe through that for a while slowly lowering the shirt and sometimes that would help.

I would also do that getting back out of the car. You would think that getting out of a stale car and into fresh air would be an improvement, but it often wouldn't - the change would almost always be bad and I would throw up.

My husband forgot my smell issues sometimes and opened the fridge. That pissed me off to no end! I cannot even tell you - I wanted to kill him.

I would lie in the bed - taking shallow little breaths trying not to throw up. I would imagine a happy place - usually a place with water because even though I hated the smell of water, *imagining* the smell of water always seemed fresh and clean.

I would be in this happy place, maybe the pond near my childhood home, floating in an inner tube while my family was hanging out nearby... and I'd be holding it together, and then it would hit me like a wall. The smell from the refrigerator - and I wouldn't have a chance to run to the bathroom. One whiff and I was retching, just hoping I was getting it on the floor and not the bedspread. Yes I kept buckets with me, but it always seemed to miss at least a bit.

I promise you, he did not forget and open that fridge often. I was livid!

There were so many things that made me sick. Getting too hot, getting a back-rub, getting a hug, driving in the car. Living… pretty much being alive made me sick.

The first trimester of pregnancy was a baptism by fire. You could sleep standing up. You crave food like a heroin addict. You then vomit up the very food you were so desperately craving. But here is what I can promise - all of it gets better.

The truth is - the reason we are such a wreck that first trimester - is that the most important stuff is happening then. We are making a heart and a brain - a nervous system and the placenta. It's all incredibly delicate - so your poor body is working very hard. You are vomiting because your body is trying to avoid any potential toxins that could at all harm your little one. You are also starving because at any moment your body is thinking, "We need a little potassium for this - demand potassium!!"

It happens so quickly and intensely and miserably - but this is it! This is motherhood. This is the beginning of you putting yourself, your whole life, on the back burner and sacrificing for someone else. And while pregnancy gets better, that sacrifice never ends.

HOUSEKEEPING IN THE FIRST TRIMESTER

That title is a joke. There is no crying in baseball and there is no housekeeping in the first trimester of pregnancy.

It's extra amusing because the nausea level is so high and your dirty house is really grossing you out. So it seems like you'd be motivated to pull out the vacuum. But that just isn't going to happen. If you are a working woman at this time you will be just as apathetic about your job.

I remember the moment when I looked at my flight schedule and knew I needed to get on a plane to Oakland because I might get called in – I would be fired immediately if I wasn't exactly where I was supposed to be and when I was supposed to be there. But getting fired seemed like a decent tradeoff for not having to get out of bed. I was ok with rolling the dice there. (Fortunately I did not get called in. Sorry Southwest Airlines!)

I guess everything that your belly is doing is highly complex and physically demanding. But to the outside world you aren't showing at all, and you just seem really whiney and lazy. Your husband is muttering about how a baby the size of a pea could possibly be so fatiguing that you can't put the cereal box away.

And you know how normally that would be a fight for sure? He has no idea how you are feeling and he has the audacity to make such a smart ass comment when you are so nauseated and exhausted…? Yeah, the problem is that you are way too tired to fight. So you roll your eyes and shuffle back onto the couch and ignore him – wishing you hadn't wasted energy on the eye roll.

I have an interesting fact for you at this point, and if you are pregnant right now I hope you really enjoy this: Did you know that (to date) no one has ANY idea how a baby "knows" how to develop?

This is truly fascinating! So we know how, for example, a heart cell works, or even how to turn a stem cell into a skin cell or lung cell. But – when your egg was fertilized and began multiplying and differentiating we have no idea what guides that.

DNA guides all sorts of thing – DNA can tell you whether you are a leader or follower, but DNA does not tell an eight celled baby to turn cell number two into the nervous system. It doesn't help decide which cells will now become brain cells and which will become nerves that sense heat or light or the flavor of good marinara sauce.

All of these incredibly complex, vital plans and details are followed out with exacting precision and as far as anyone can tell the mechanism of chemicals turning cells into this or that has zero guiding process. Think about that!

Mankind has seen with telescopes to the ends of the galaxy, we know where on the DNA code that it says some of us can't stand Cilantro, we have even created music programs that can tell you which songs we would like to hear.

We know so much about the human body and mind and universe, but in every single living animal we do not know the process that directs the early development. Isn't that just magic!! A part of me hopes that they never ever figure it out. It's too beautiful.

It's like that scientist that found two snowflakes that were identical. I wanted to kick her in the teeth. Really?? We have lived with this wonder that all the gazillions of gajillions (those are real numbers!) of snowflakes that had fallen to the earth throughout all of time and as far as we knew no two had ever been identical. The awe and mystery of that! What a world!!

Then "little miss know it all" had to come out and

say, "Oh! I found two identical snowflakes!" Well bite me lady. (By the way if you google it the 'identical pair' has been redacted... mostly.) I intend, for the rest of my life, to decide that this means that there still have never been two identical snowflakes, and therefore I will enjoy my joyous mystery and hide my eyes if anyone attempts to kill my happiness.

Well, as awesome as snowflakes are... – the fact that our knowledge of time and space, of quarks and neutrinos, of nuclear fission and iPhone apps – has yet to uncover what process directs the early development of your little baby - that wonder, and mystery blows unique snowflakes out of the water!

No matter how difficult this pregnancy (and life) gets – remember that there is a poetry, a song beneath it all, that will move you to tears if you will embrace it. And this bit of wonder going on inside of you just touches on it! It is a glimpse at the brushstrokes of God, and I hope you will choose to take the moment of awe!!

So back to your un-vacuumed living room and nasty shower and dank mouth with teeth that keep not getting brushed. All I can tell you is that this fatigue will pass and in the second trimester you have a whole lot more energy.

Even I did, and I was a sick as a dog. I just went around town with plenty of energy, throwing up. Not normal, but I was up and around soon after the second trimester settled in.

It's only going to be this truly exhausting for this one trimester... granted, I am telling you that we are just going to throw a couple of months of your life away on being completely unproductive. But – what we forget is that you are actually being very very productive. The fundamental blocks of your baby and his entire future are being formed. The more you drain yourself at this time, the more you are draining a body that is working on jobs of the utmost importance.

Those ancient mother-goddess images of female creators forming the world... that's you dank, nasty mouth!! That's you.

ABOUT THAT SPITTING: PTALYSIS

Remember how I mentioned the spitting?? It was another bizarre symptom, which, I'll tell you; I have never met any other woman who shared this one. But thank God for the Internet where I was able to chat with other fellow spitters. Fun times!

For those of you who joined me in the more intense end of the 'morning sickness' scale you may have also experienced Ptalysis (that is the constant need to spit).

Here's a semi-related question... have you heard that you need to drink 8 glasses of water per day - and that if you aren't drinking 8 glasses of water per day that you are actually dehydrated? And was some part of you amazed that you have been wandering around your whole life thinking you were healthy as could be, but discovered that you were actually balancing on the brink of dehydration all this time because you have never in your life had 8 glasses of water in a day??

How about the fact that tea and caffeinated soda are actually dehydrating and yet you drink them when you are thirsty?? Have you heard that statistic?? Well - prepare to have your mind blown!!

I lived on nothing but strong black tea and Pepsi for months! Months I tell you! I should be dead, I am a walking miracle!

Either that, or maybe "experts" aren't 100% experts on everything. Ptalysis has to be dehydrating because, after all, I spit about every 5 seconds... all day long.

With my first pregnancy the spitting lasted only a couple of weeks, and with my third pregnancy it lasted about two and a half months. But with my second pregnancy... ah that horrible pregnancy, it lasted the entire time. In fact, it lasted for about thirty minutes after that delivery.

For a few moments after my daughter was born, and I was out of my mind in pain and stress and drama (you will just love this story!) and I remember looking at my son and my husband and the nurses and the new baby, and then looking desperately for somewhere to spit.

Ptalysis was so humiliating. I had a cup with me at all times and I would slowly take sips of very, very, strong black tea so that I could swallow. That would work for an hour or two until I was so full of tea I couldn't take it anymore. Then I would get a disposable cup of some kind and I would start spitting. That would last for hours.

Run errands, take my son to preschool, spit into the cup, talk to his teacher, between sentences, spit in the cup, pull out of the parking lot - throw up in the weeds, drive to the store - spit in the cup. Talk with a neighbor - keep spitting in a cup, throw up in a garbage can... spit in the cup, finally get "empty" enough and brew some super strong black tea - toss the cup of spit - and start sipping the black tea.

That was every single minute of every day. I promise... I promise, I promise, IpromiseIpromiseIpromise that I really, truly am NOT crazy.

I slept on towels at night with my mouth open so that the spit could just... well, I'm sure you get the idea. Isn't it weird that my husband wasn't sexually attracted to me at this time?? Remember how grateful I was that I wasn't randy during my pregnancies... do you understand why that was a blessing now?

So, while I did manage to survive on tea and soda, I am not at all suggesting that you do the same. Just because it was survivable as a matter of living, doesn't mean that it's a great idea.

I will admit that while the vomiting was depressing, Ptalysis was depressing in a way that even vomiting didn't touch.

At least when you are sick and running off to throw up, people feel sorry for you and assume that you're not going out of your way to gross them out. The spitting is a much harder sell in the sympathy department.

I remember calling one of my girlfriends and breaking down while I was on the phone with her. I just couldn't imagine living with it any more. I did eventually find a doctor who thought he could help and he prescribed me a drug that had helped some women before. I ran into a tiny pharmacy in the small mountain town where we were living. When the pharmacist took the prescription, I wrote a note to him (couldn't talk… spit and no cup) - asking him to make sure that the drug was a class "B" medication.

He was very confused by my writing a note instead of speaking, but he rolled with it ok. I am so grateful that I was at a small pharmacy where they actually had the time to talk with each patient one on one, because he thought the drug looked fine initially - but recognized that it was a combination pill that had several ingredients and then he went through each ingredient individually and found that the drug belladonna was included.

Belladonna is not a class "B" drug.

If you have a medical condition while you are pregnant getting to know what a 'class B' drug is should be part of your new momma education. Class "B" means that while they never ever test drugs on pregnant women, it has been used by pregnant women without ever showing any adverse effects on the baby. Tylenol is used constantly during pregnancy and it will never be given a rating higher than class "B" because it is just too unthinkable to do any sort of study on pregnant women and the possible adverse effects of drugs on their babies.

If a drug is class "B" it is as safe as can possibly be known and observed for the mother and baby. My daughter may have turned out just fine had I taken that drug, but having missed out on 4 months of spitting would not have been worth it if it meant risking her health. It was miserable, no doubt - but I am so very glad that I asked him instead of just taking the prescription, and I am so glad that he was patient and thorough.

I'm sharing this because I think it's important to realize that your responsibility as a mother starts before you may realize. That if you have any doubts or concerns you shouldn't be afraid to voice them, and to speak up.

Ptalysis may have been humiliating, and it was, but four months of humiliation was totally worth the shame knowing I didn't risk her health for my pride...

So what? So I delivered my middle child while still spitting into a towel. So what if the nurses in the delivery room were asking my husband what I was doing? Who cares if they all thought I was crazy. Have I told you that I'm not? I'm really not - I'm just really lousy at pregnancy.

SECOND TRIMESTER

I'm not fat - really!

Now, for most women, the "just fat" phase happens in the first trimester. For me - due to the hyper-emesis, it wasn't until the end of the second - although with each baby my tummy popped out faster than the one before. My mother, on the other hand, who had perfect pregnancies and seemed to just sail through the 9 months, seemed to hit the "just fat" phase immediately.

Her face puffed up almost before she knew she was pregnant and she would complain that she was only 8 weeks along with a baby the size of a strawberry, but she was 20 pounds heavier already.

It's always different, but the truth is that no matter who you are you will hit the place where no one looking at you would know that you are pregnant, but you're a whole lot bigger than you were.

It's awkward. I remember wishing that there was a tee-shirt I could wear that would say, "I'm not fat... just pregnant."

Nothing to be done about it though. Just go with it, because after the baby is born you are right back there again except then you are sleep deprived and stinking of sour mild AND you look fat. And the phrase, "I'm not fat - I just WAS pregnant..." doesn't look as cool on a tee shirt, plus your boobs won't fit into the shirt anyway.

FINDING OUT THE SEX

Obviously this is a very personal decision - but if you don't find out the sex of your baby in the fifth month then you are a bad person and have already started off parenting as a failure.

That was a joke.

But really - you need to go ahead and find out - otherwise we don't know what to buy you, and your baby will be born with nothing but yellow stuff to wear. I am speaking from experience here. We refused to tell anyone what we were having with my first son and we have way too many photos of him in ducky onesies. The first year of his life I had a million conversations with strangers about my "cute, little... um... is it a boy or a girl?"

Originally, we decided not to find out with our first - we had the ultrasound tech put the sex in an envelope and decided we would wait to open it until we were ready... that lasted about as long as it took us to pull out from the doctor's office and onto the highway. My husband said he couldn't take it anymore, and to just open it. I did and saw the words, "Looks like a boy!"

I read those words and we both lost it. He pulled off the side of the freeway and we both cried. I was afraid it would take away some of the fun - but from my experience, the day I found out the sex of each one of my babies is branded into my mind much like the days that they were born. It made for one more moment in my life that I was knocked over with joy.

With my middle daughter we were torn between thinking that we were pretty good with raising a boy and would like to do it again, and the desire for something different than what we had known. When we were told it was a girl we were so excited! I kept looking at the ultrasound image to try make sure, but the longer the ultrasound tech and I chatted about the image the more uncomfortable my husband got. Within a few minutes he told us to cut it out and quit talking about her lady parts. He had been the father of a girl for only a couple minutes and he was already protective.

My last child was just about due for the "find out the gender" appointment when my son was admitted to the hospital with appendicitis. When he was finally able to get up and move (post-surgery) we decided to cheer him up by heading to the ultrasound lab to see if we were having a baby brother or sister.

She was a sister.

He was hoping for a little brother.

He tried not to let on, but he was bummed. The chance to see her and her little hands and face as she rolled around in my tummy seemed to cheer him up and he soon was excited just to watch her dancing around in there. He seemed to decide it was ok to have a baby sister joining us since she was so cute. And I am so glad that we had the memory of finding out she was a girl. It made her birth all the more exciting.

While earlier my son and daughter had been arguing back and forth hoping for either a girl or boy before we found out, having that knowledge allowed them to just get excited to have their sister coming.

The day that our youngest was born we had them both in the room with us.

(You are judging me right now, aren't you? You're thinking, 'What kinda granola hippy am I reading who would have her kids in the room watching that bloody display?' I assure you, we didn't. We had them slip behind the curtain for the exams and pushing yuckyness!!)

They watched me walk around during labor and argued about who would get to hold her first. (To be honest most of the time I was in labor was the middle of the night and they all were sleeping - but - you know - moral support and whatnot.)

On her very first night I tucked my son into bed and then laid his brand spankin' new baby sister on his chest. His face crumpled up and he asked me what I was going to do?

I was baffled. I had no clue what my little guy meant. He said I needed to figure out what I was going to do because he was never ever going to give her back.

I know - right?

I not only got to watch him revel in being a brother (and not worry about wanting a brother) - I got to see the father he will someday be... a truly great one.

LIFE CONTINUES

The thing that I think the second trimester makes you realize is just how much 'life goes on' despite all that you are experiencing. It just does.

You are having conversations with people while you are being kicked in the spleen. I worked towards the end of my first pregnancy as a flight attendant and I'd be stumbling around in turbulence or helping someone with a soda and have to go vomit or try not to pee when I was kicked in the bladder.

All sorts of stuff comes up while you are pregnant, and it is sometimes overwhelming to be dealing with it all at once.

I lost my Mom while I was pregnant. My son got appendicitis when I was pregnant. My kids had school, or the flu or swim lessons. My husband got a new job and we moved and all of this happened while

I was sick and scared and living in this odd altered reality.

FEELING THE BABY MOVE!

I saved the best part of the second trimester for last because this is the one and only part of pregnancy that I didn't hate. This is the miracle of feeling your baby moving inside of you. Nothing in the world can make up for the totally unfair disparity in nature between men and women.

Getting to live an extra decade doesn't even come close. But - this little bit of time - the months that you spend with a little person tucked safe and sound in your tummy, feeling him wiggle and kick and jump... it is an awesome, wondrous experience! And men never will know this joy. Take a small moment to revel in that... it's only one thing – only one benefit in a world of drawbacks - but it is a doozy.

It takes a while before you notice the movement with your first. I think you are feeling the baby for a while, but you've been so nauseated and gassy that you have just been assuming that it was all that you were feeling. Eventually it gets strong enough and obvious enough and it dawns on you just what's going on... it's awesome!

I did something with my first pregnancy that I have never heard of anyone else doing. I got my tummy really cold - (just left my tummy bare in a cold room), and then I would set my hands on one side of my tummy and wait. Slowly a hard lump would develop under my hands. Then I would move my hands to the other side of my tummy and wait. The hard lump would shift over to there. It was wonderful. I did this for over an hour. It was heaven, and even though I couldn't feel any movement yet at all, it was so nice to think that we were already cuddling!!!

There is a downside to feeling the baby kicking. It gets stronger.

The first month or two of movement is so sweet. But eventually you start getting beat up. It goes from a pleasant fluttering in your tummy to a mighty war being waged against your spine... and bladder, and spleen and ribs and a bunch of other stuff that feels pretty important when it gets punched.

However, for most of the second trimester the movement is subtle enough to just enjoy - but don't get too comfortable. That mighty war is coming and it's only weeks away!

THIRD TRIMESTER

Sleepless.

The third trimester begins fine enough, but by the end you have regressed. You are peeing constantly again.

Constantly.

At some point in those last couple of months you will also no longer be able to sleep. It is a mix of having to pee all of the time - the baby deciding that nighttime is 'par-tay' time, and your husband trying to wake you to make you stop snoring.

I might snore every once in a while, but from what I am told, I snore like crazy that last trimester. I would have said that it was impossible, as I swear I never actually slept, but since I assume my husband is not a liar I must have gotten some sleep.

The baby is also huge at this point. I remember pulling my maternity top up and pulling the big nasty elasto-waist thing from my maternity shorts down and just letting my big huge belly hang out one night. I was staring at the TV when I heard my husband make a weird noise. I looked over at him and he was staring at my belly. The baby was rolling around making huge waves move back and forth across my stomach. He looked up at me and said, "I feel like I'm on drugs or something - that looks insane!" It's funny to think: for the world around you, the world inside of you is totally foreign.

For other women, third trimester sleeplessness involves leg cramps - which are horrendous. I only had one cramp in all three pregnancies.

I have spent a ridiculous portion of my life feeling very sorry for myself and my dramatic miserable months of pregnancy, but that one leg cramp was enough to make me realize that I was not to be pitied... well, not to be AS pitied anyway. Those things suck!

There are so many ways to be miserable when pregnant. Acid reflux, varicose veins, incontinence, leg cramps, hemorrhoids. Every single woman has some issues, and it is easy for me to think that mine were the worst - but that leg cramp told me to shut my pie hole. I didn't have it as bad as I could have.

PREPARING FOR CHILDBIRTH

Here's my theory on preparing for childbirth. Don't.

Seriously - this is like preparing for a train wreck. Just put your head down and hold the heck on. You will get through it - but it will not be easy.

BIRTH PLANS

I have talked to women who have had horrible deliveries - and really smooth awesome deliveries and I have yet to find much of a correlation between their birth plans and their outcomes.

It appears to me that some women have better hips and such for childbirth and that can make a real difference, some have fewer pain receptors in their nether regions and that seems to make a difference, some have good pain management plans - which also seem to help, some also have epidurals and those help a lot.

What doesn't help is making a big dream plan and getting too attached to it. It will go how it goes. If your baby is breech and you need a C-section - so what? If your baby is upside down and causes terrible back labor pain, or your hips are too small or you aren't dilating or whatever - it is what it is.

Childbirth is a big friggin' deal. We are talking about a process, between pregnancy and childbirth, that killed about a third of women just a couple hundred years ago. Really.

I think we hate the thought that we would not have been survivors. I had that thought with the hyper-emesis - I may not have survived pregnancy had I not lived in the modern world. If I had survived, it would have done far more horrific things to my body from the extent of the malnutrition and dehydration. (My teeth would have been rotten!)

Many, many women once died during childbirth. It is a risky venture and while in our day and age it is very safe, realize that we are not talking about getting a haircut and think of how much can go wrong with that!

I know all the baby books tell you to make a plan, but I do not see the point of it. Or at least don't get very attached to it. Nothing will go the way you planned and that's ok - so decide that you will take it moment by moment, trust your instincts, listen to your husband, your midwife or doctor and be ok with whatever comes.

I am confident that the one thing you don't need on that day is stress - and you will be a whole lot more stressed if you are trying to control things and follow a plan, than if you let it go.

HERE'S MY TAKE ON PAIN MANAGEMENT

Lamaze - I never did it - and never did any other birth coaching, hypno-birthing etc. I was just too sick to sit through a class for most of the pregnancy, and I also knew there was no way my husband was going to go to one of those things with me and going alone would be weird.

K- he read this, and he says he would have - but, I think I know him better than he does… really. The guy he is today probably would have… the twenty-six year old who tried to sell me on going to burning man when I was past my due date and there was no cell phone coverage… that guy was not Lamaze class friendly, and I pick my battles.

So - I'm sure it would make for a hilarious story that would be fun to write about - but unfortunately I never did it.

Epidurals: I had them with two of the three deliveries. They are awesome!

It is important to note here that I am biased as my husband does these for a living so I had no intention of ever having a baby without one. But in both deliveries, once I got the epidural I had zero pain. Zero.

I had no problems pushing. Loved it!

But I also know that there are anesthesia providers who aren't great at epidural placement. If you get a rock star as an anesthesia provider then you are set. If you get someone who isn't all that skilled, it might not go as well.

If you do get an epidural make sure you are left sitting up a bit. Lying down completely flat can cause low blood pressure and really mess you up. Another thing - the epidural is one of the safest medical procedures in modern life. The injection is actually below your spinal cord, but there is always a risk in every single medical procedure and so epidurals have potential complications too. Make sure you research your options before the big day.

CHECKING OUT OF THE HOSPITAL

I never did this either. As someone who never once had maternity insurance, I set up a payment plan and tried to have a percentage paid before each delivery so as to receive a discount. That's all of any of the hospitals I had seen before I delivered... the financial office.

Packing: So you are packing your bag for items to take to the hospital and wondering, "What do I need?"

Nothing!

Just kidding.

You need a car seat - that's really important - do not show up without one.

You also will need some clothes to go home in - cute as those hospital gowns are they'd charge you $2,000 if you take them home... seriously they would. I always brought clothes that I was wearing well into the second trimester to wear home. After all, I thought, there was no way that, having delivered the baby, they wouldn't fit.

They totally didn't fit.

It was really embarrassing. I looked like a marshmallow in a strait jacket.

You also need a onesie and a blanket for the baby.

That's about it though. I would not bring soothing mantra music - people do it - I wouldn't. People bring all sorts of things, candles and whatnot.

But this is my thought, especially if you decide to forgo anesthesia - once you are in the last stages of labor everything in that room is an annoying, irritating, distraction. I mean everything. Your husband, the nurse, the strings on the pajamas... all of it was invented to deliberately annoy you.

And your soothing chanting music will be as useful as it would have been on a roller coaster. That is the best possible analogy I have for childbirth. Picture yourself on a roller coaster. That first part where you are climbing up the big, big hill. That is where people ask you how much it hurts and you think you're a champ, it hurts but it really doesn't feel that bad!

Then you crest that hill and all hell breaks loose.

The beautiful meadow and hill, all the plans to go to your happy place and hum or whatever - that's all trashed and all you are doing is holding on waiting for the ride to end.

Now, like I said, I have seen women who didn't seem to experience as much pain - in fact I have a friend who couldn't even tell if she was having a baby. Honestly. She would only realize it when she had a baby crowning and she could sense the pressure. This is a true story! But that is just the reality. We are all on a bell curve in how painful childbirth is.

Here's hoping you're on the fun end.

BRAXTON HICKS CONTRACTIONS

Braxton Hicks tend to begin around this time with your first pregnancy, but it's different with each woman and each pregnancy. By my third pregnancy I was having them in the very first months. True story - still not crazy.

Part of why you don't feel them until the last trimester with your first pregnancy is that you have no idea what they will feel like. Almost everyone I know had a strange, miraculous moment where they realized that they had been having them; they just hadn't realized that "that" was what they were. So, if you're on your first pregnancy and are in your third trimester and don't think you've ever had a Braxton hicks contraction, I may just give you that weird moment right now...!

Contractions do NOT feel like a squeezing sensation. They actually feel like your tummy is pushing out. Inflating... Did that make sense?

When you first start feeling the contractions you will think that the baby is stretching. That they have their back pressed against your tummy and that they are pushing out. Can you picture that? The feet and hands are against your spine and they are pressing. That is what it feels like. And when you feel that "baby pressing" sensation, you will notice that your belly gets hard.

That is not the baby pushing against you - that is a contraction!

I KNOW!! It's not at all what you thought right?? Glad I could be the person to share this moment with you. Now, here's the good news. It's not that bad right? Not that big of a deal! You can deal with that - and it will get more intense, but you are already dealing with it!!

The bad part?? You may have felt a sharp stabbing pain in your lady parts. I'm not positive, but that feeling has something to do with your cervix dilating... and that is part of labor too. (Insert your choice of sad face emoticon here.)

GETTING BIG

The other problem with the third trimester is that you are huge. You thought you were huge in the first trimester. Remember that? When you worried that the 10-15 pounds you'd gained made you look fat? Now you have tripled that and it's in the form of a gigantic belly.

Your center of gravity is shot and your hips are made of Jell-O. You can't just walk around, and instead you do this weird, spread-legged waddle. Sharp pains keep stabbing your hips, your legs are swollen, your girly parts are swollen. Every inch of you aches. I remember my back just killing me - but you can't stretch! At all.

Here is another special moment that will happen, as has happened to a million other mothers' before you, and you will join our special club once this moment has occurred.

You will drop something.

That's kind of it.

You will drop it - and the thought will run through your head - I wonder who is picking that up? It sure isn't going to be you - is it?

You will debate if it is really all that necessary. You can grab another spoon, or pencil, or book. And you will just be a bit resigned, and comfortable with the idea that this thing might just stay on the floor for all of eternity. Because no matter what inconvenience is facing you, it's not so inconvenient that you are interested in trying to squat down to retrieve your item.

(This will get more difficult with subsequent pregnancies when the thing that requires you squatting to retrieve it - is you first child.)

WAITING

My friend once said that pregnancy is 8 months followed by a year. That last month just never ever ends. Every woman starts to prepare for immanent delivery at about 36 weeks. After all, 37 weeks counts as full term. It could be any day!

'Any day!' NEVER ends. Most women actually go a few days to even a couple of weeks past their due date. That is like standing at the top of the high dive and knowing that at any moment someone is going to shove you in... For over a month.

And every time you talk to a friend or family member they all say the same thing, "Any news??"

It actually starts to feel embarrassing. As though you made the whole pregnancy up. As though you are just faking it. Like one day you will have to call everyone up and admit that this whole pregnancy thing was all in your mind. After all, how on earth has it been 6 weeks since we all started expecting that we were running to the hospital at any minute?

So pack that bag and make your plans. It's fun to plan and imagine and prepare. It is so fun! Just be ready to throw all those plans out the window when the time comes and enjoy that day for the miracle that it is, because you will never ever experience a more magical moment then the day you bring your babies into the world.

THE BIG DAY

I thought I'd give you a run-down of my childbirth experiences. I hope you like them; every single person's birth story goes down as one of the most profound days of their entire lives. And if for no greater reason than that - they are worth telling.

BIG BROTHER'S STORY

My first child was born with what my husband called, 'The Cadillac of Births.' We were a couple of days overdue and so we scheduled an induction.

My mom was visiting and as we headed out in the wee hours, she was tidying up our tiny apartment and making sure we had everything.

We got to the hospital and started the Pitocin. The nurses asked me to rate my pain from one to ten. I said '3' knowing that they were all in awe of my pain management skills. I know they are used to whiney, weak, women, but I am going to blow their minds with my cool, proud, childbirth. After all I had such a horrible pregnancy, my ability to suffer has got to be amazing at this point!

The doctor decided I was progressing slowly so he broke my water. After his clever plastic hook thing had done its job he headed out and some friends of ours came in to visit us. Two contractions after that I was on fire. I had no idea it was going to hurt like that! It took my breath away. My husband and friend were chatting and within a few minutes I went from laughing with them to trying to control the tears running down my cheeks. They looked over at me with a "What the heck happened?" expression.

I was clearly NOT going to put on some display of courage and Zen power. I was going down hard. My husband was preparing to attend anesthesia school soon, so he had no qualms about encouraging me to get a needle in my back.

That epidural was pure heaven! And, this is another random woman who holds a profound place in my heart. I still remember her face too.

She was Asian, had glasses - and to this day I love her. She saved me. There is nothing better than NOT being in pain. I did then start feeling a little freaked out about the total paralysis of my legs. But not too bad - I wasn't ready to go back to a lower body nervous system any time soon.

As soon as the pain left I was fully dilated. And it took me a bit to figure out how to push with no feeling?? This is a real risk with having a good strong epidural.

(Here's what no one is telling you - it's just like pooping. I was trying to find some nether region - something like stomach crunches that would be "pushing." No - if you can't feel "how" to push - just pretend you're pooping and you've got it.) Sorry, that's nasty, but that's all it is.

The entire labor lasted for several hours, but the "pushing phase" was less than 1 hour. And then there was a big commotion as the doctor showed up (he didn't come in until right at that last push).

This is an important point: - if you think your OBGYN will play a huge roll on that day you're probably wrong. Some random nurse, who you have no ability to pick, will be assigned to you on that day, and he or she will be the person who most affects you experience. If there is something that I can argue is wrong with the medical system we have today, this would be one of those things. The nurse who will be helping you through the most important day of your life should be a person you can choose. They can make that day wonderful or horrible and you get no say in choosing them, and their ability to please patients has little to no impact on their pay. I was lucky, I had great nurses, but I know people who did not. This is also a reason to go the route of a nurse midwife instead of an OBGYN. They tend to stay for the entire process – not just the last couple of pushes. I still chose an OB – I liked having the surgeon right there in case it was necessary, but I see a great argument for nurse-midwifes too.

After I finally got the hang of it - it wasn't long. A couple of good pushes.

And then there was a cry.

I cannot describe the awe and wonder. There are not words - truly.

I was so glad to see him! And he looked so much like my husband... which even with all the adrenaline and joy - seemed a little weird.

And when I heard that first cry - it was so good to know that he was ok...

but...

then he didn't stop crying.

He just kept crying! I remember looking at the medical staff and wondering if I was supposed to be doing something?? Was he going to stop? Would he do this forever? I remember kind of patting him and saying, "It's ok..." over and over. I suddenly felt totally out of my league.

My husband leaned down to give me a kiss. We were crying and laughing - overwhelmed with emotion, and in a sweet quiet voice he whispered, "You really got jacked up!"

That's true. That's my guy. Biggest moment of our lives - and he thought I should know that I was ripped apart down there, you know, since I couldn't feel it.

It took a long time, but our son did eventually stop crying. My husband and I were totally obsessed with him. We did not let anyone take him.

If they wanted to weigh or measure, or give shots or circumcise, then they had to do it right next to me, or else my husband went with him. There was no sleeping in the nursery, nothing. I don't know if we were paranoid about accidentally going home with the wrong baby, or if we were just too in love to be apart.

This was the only pregnancy in which I spent the night at the hospital.

That night I experienced a little miracle.

I remember waking up in the middle of the night with that weird feeling that only happens a few times in your life. You know that something big has happened and it all hits you as you come back to consciousness. I opened my eyes and looked over at my son. He was awake. My baby boy was staring right at me! Just kinda curious. Not crying at all. Staring right at me. It was the most wonderful feeling.

BABY SISTER'S STORY

I'm going to skip now to my third child's birth, and there is a reason for this. Let's just put a pin in that for now...

With my third child I was fully aware of the fact that I was going to have a strange and fast labor so I didn't mess around. I had been having contractions forever - and I was still more than two weeks from my due date, but the contractions were getting intense. I was sitting at my son's soccer practice visiting with another mom and breathing through contractions.

I decided that we were heading to the hospital as soon as practice was over. I told my husband that if they checked me and I was dilated to a 3 we would go home, but if I was a 4 we were staying.

We got in the room and had me checked... 3 1/2. Of course.

So I made the call. I wasn't leaving. I knew I could keep the contractions going as long as I walked. And so the kids and my fella all snuggled down in the maternity room while I started walking the halls. I would walk and bounce as much as I could to keep those contractions rolling, and every hour or so I had the nurse check my progress. As long as I kept moving I kept gaining about a half a centimeter an hour.

All night long I kept it up, and I waited until I was at an 8 1/2. I got my epidural. Score! Then it was time to push.

We woke up the kids and told them to hang out with a nurse back behind a curtain. I really love that we kept the kids with us. They were so excited about getting their new sister and so the time that they spent with me while I was laboring and listening to the heartbeat, watching the monitor, being there listening to the actual delivery was awesome. Yes - I know - I'm such a hippie. But it really was awesome.

Two pushes. That's right - two. Because I'll tell you what - once your uterus has done this a couple of times it gets strong! This was the only baby that I didn't tear too badly with. With her being only 37 1/2 weeks she weighed only a bit over 6 lbs. A few ounces make a huge difference.

When I was covered back up and most of the blood and mess was rushed away; big brother and big sister climbed right into the bed with me and the baby. They were so thrilled. It was such an amazing, beautiful time, and while I understand that most families don't plan it as such a family affair - I'm glad we did.

Want to know how I talked my husband into this family style birth? I just didn't make any plans.

That way when the big day came I was like: "Surprise - the kids are coming with us." Yes, he thought I was weird - but it was a little late to start calling people. Plus, I think he liked the idea too.

THE SORDID TALE OF THE MIDDLE-IST

So here we are dear reader, I am ready to tell you one of the greatest stories of my entire life. The birth of my second.

Here is the one good reason to forgo anesthesia: It makes for a much better birth story. Births with anesthetic are elegant. There are tears and hugging and beauty. Births without anesthesia are dramatic, awful, horrible, traumas. But, that's the reality about awful things - they make for much better stories. Pain and suffering are a part of life for a reason. We live for happiness and comfort, but we learn and grow from pain. Pain makes memories. You do not forget the lessons it teaches. So while I would never ever do it again – if I hadn't had this anesthetic free birth, I wouldn't have this story… So - there's always that.

We had just moved to a new house days earlier and the house was full of boxes.

My Mom had just died. (Sorry, I know that's a bummer, but she had.) I had moved across several states to live near my Mom and within weeks of my moving she died.

Now, I was in a new town, no friends, no furniture, no mom, nothing even really unpacked. I went to the local Wal-Mart, (the only major store in our small town at the time) and looked for baby stuff. I bought a cheap crib, but the only crib bedding was primary colored Winnie the Pooh. I'm no great fashionista, I'm not really able to put together an outfit that doesn't involve jeans as a starting point - but the Winnie the Pooh bedding was not going to cut it for my new baby girl.

So I bought a hot glue gun and some fabric.

This is truly bizarre behavior. I am the least creative, crafty, woman I know. I still can't bake a boxed cake to this day. But, I spent two days hot glue gunning a curtain, a bumper, a blanket, pillows, and making a beautiful little bedroom set for her. It really turned out pretty well. Truly - with nothing but fabric and a hot glue gun.

I was so proud of myself. My husband was laughing while he took pictures of me. My belly was so huge that it stuck out from under the tops that I was wearing. I was just sitting spread legged on the floor of our rental with the hot glue gun, big bare belly and brown and pink fabric between my legs.

Then, I cleaned the truck. I wanted a baby to come home in a clean truck.

This obviously sounds very "nesting-ish" right? But we had just moved - so it was also just necessary, and I was still a few days early so I wasn't overly suspicious.

I had been having Braxton Hicks contractions for most of the pregnancy; I was having them that day too. No pattern - just random contractions, they were getting more painful - but no pattern. I told my husband, "Hey, these kinda hurt - it's possible that we might have a baby tonight." He told me that we'd better not because he had a difficult surgery in the morning and needed his sleep. He was joking.

No - he wasn't - he was serious.

I stayed up late talking to my sister-in-law and trying to decide if I needed to go to the hospital. I was still having strong contractions, but they were so irregular. I called the Doctor and asked him.

No. No baby.

I didn't have a labor pattern...

He said that I could, of course, come in if I wanted, but no pattern means no baby.

They got worse. I threw up and lost my plug. (Don't know what that is?? Look that one up! Good times!)

So much fun.

I woke up my husband and my doctor. Clarified that yes there was still no pattern - I checked the timing and went over 20 minutes without a single contraction - both men are clear that no one has a baby if they aren't having contractions for over 20 minutes.

I admit they are probably right.

Now it was about 2 am and I got into a bathtub hoping it would help with the discomfort. I had a contraction and although I was trying to breathe through it, it was killing me. I was gripping the tub so hard that I was shaking. That's when it hit me - there is NO WAY a Braxton Hicks contraction can possibly hurt that bad.

I jumped out of the tub and ran my bare bottom into the bedroom.

Do you recall my description of how horrendous my bottom looked at this point??

Picture me - I was soaking wet, huge, dimply fat, pregnant and buck-naked and pissed. SO- SO- SO PISSED!! I can't tell you the exact words, but they were along the lines of what kind of *&(^*&# is in bed sleeping while I am having a baby in the $#@#$* bathtub?!?!?

He yelled at me!

There is a part of me that will never, ever, ever, forgive him for that decision.

I then started screaming and crying... something along the lines of getting screamed at while I'm having a baby, and then I have another contraction, and I need to push - bad.

I say it... or more like I mutter it...

"Oh no! I need to push!"

Then he FREAKS!

I had no bag packed yet - I had pulled a bag out a couple of days ago and set a couple of things near it - most of our stuff was still in boxes. He started throwing stuff into the bag. When I unpacked the bag a week later I was laughing so hard – there was the weirdest stuff in there.

I remember for a few seconds becoming calm and looking at this really nasty rental house carpet and pondering the reality that my baby would be born on that stuff. I was not going to do this on my bed that was for sure.

Somehow, while I was plotting the carpets destruction, my husband had thrown our 4-year-old boy, and a bag of who knows what into our shiny new Volvo, pulled a dress over my head (no panties), and half carried me to the car. I brought a towel to keep spitting in.

He drove 110 miles per hour through deer heaven trying to get to the hospital. I remember trying not to push for a couple of contractions. The pain was so insane I just couldn't believe I was alive. It could not be humanly possible to hurt this bad and be alive.

I remember looking at the side of the door. I was holding onto the 'oh-shoot' handle that sits above the door and I would pull up on it and clench my dimply behind trying not to push as the contraction hit. I would look at the side of the door and wonder, 'If I hit my head against it hard enough, could I knock myself out?' It wasn't just a viable option at the moment, it was hope.

Then... the police.

Seriously.

Suddenly, we had a police car with full lights and sirens blaring, following us at 110. Hubby put on the emergency flashers and we kept racing along ignoring the cop.

When we entered the town another police car flew in front of us and stopped right in front of our car cutting us off. My husband slammed on the breaks narrowly missing the cop and screamed out the window that we were having a baby. Somehow they got the gist and yelled that they would escort us.

So there we were. This is true. Middle of the night - two cop cars with lights and sirens blaring and a Volvo all careening towards the hospital. I was screaming and plotting my ability to knock myself out against the side of the door. My son was screaming in the back - (such trauma for a little guy) - while my husband was screaming to our son that it was ok and that Mommy was just fine.

We pulled into the hospital. I was in mid contraction as the door flew open and a nurse asked me to get out of the car. I screamed, "I can't get out!" To which she replied, "(Big audible sigh) Yes... you can."

Apparently screaming, dramatic, women in mid-childbirth are a bit annoying to your graveyard shift maternity nurses. What she didn't seem to get was that there was a head crowning between my legs and that if I stood up it would just fall out.

The cops were a little less irritated with the annoying, birthing woman and they reached in and grabbed my semi-naked body and threw me into the waiting wheel chair.

With a husband in anesthesia I knew I wasn't getting any help for what I needed to do. In our rural area the anesthesia providers are as much as 20 minutes away from the hospital when they are on call. And they never call them when someone is this far along. I knew it.

But I asked anyway. I told my husband that I was going to kill him if I had to do this without anesthesia - he obediently asked if they could get one of the nurse anesthetists to come in, but I knew the truth - it was too late. I was facing a horrible, horrible, reality. I begged the nurse – "Please give me something - anything - give me a Tylenol!"

How sad is that? - I begged for that Tylenol. But it was never going to happen.

I was going to do this - right now - and no one had anything that could help me.

The nurses still seemed to be of the opinion that I

was being awfully melodramatic but all that changed when they decided to take a peak between my legs. They were trying to put those stupid baby monitors around my tummy and get some gloves and a bunch of other "nurse stuff."

My medically trained, genius, husband was holding our son and yelling random stuff along with them. Another contraction was coming and I knew there was only one way to get the pain to stop. But I didn't want to do it. In the worst way - I so badly didn't want to do it.

I made the most pitiful attempt to hit someone - by taking a very loopy swing at my husband's face and looked him in the eye and told him, "I hate you," and then reached down with my hands and...

I did it.

It was awful. I tore so badly I had stitches all the way up in my behindo-holeyo. Seriously.

After I delivered her head the yelling got even worse. My husband was yelling, "There's a head - there's a head!" The nurses were yelling at one another about who should do what and why they were both screwing up - but they were both still messing with monitors and gel and gloves and whatnot. One of them finally came over and helped to deliver her shoulders. And that was that.

In case you are wondering... this is the best way to describe the pain: If I took a baseball bat and I swung with everything I had - as hard as I could, and hit you in the head. It wouldn't hurt as bad as those contractions.

And if I took that bat and I just kept doing it again and again... that still wouldn't be adequate to explain the kind of pain I am describing. To this day it does not seem possible to me that a person can feel that much pain and not die.

MY THOUGHTS ON "NATURE"

So - this is the only thing I can say for "natural" childbirth.

There is nothing natural about it. You are ripping something the size of a watermelon out of a hole the size of an almond. There are women who are bigger and so the size of the hole is bigger relative to the baby - so sure - maybe it's not as painful for them - but it's still not the size of a watermelon. Even for taller women this is still not an acceptable size discrepancy.

The idea that ripping your vagina apart without anesthesia is the "natural" way to do it is ridiculous. My friend who is a physician put it this way: You will likely need your wisdom teeth pulled in your life... should you do that "naturally?" You will need to have surgery for different ailments in life... should you ask that these surgeries be performed "naturally?" When you feel that you are no longer wanting to have more children your husband may get a vasectomy... should he do that 'naturally?'

In no other place in life if I had said that I was going to need to rip my body apart - much less tear one of the most sensitive parts of my body apart would there be pressure to go through that experience "naturally."

If that is your thing - good for you. But it's about time women stop judging one another with the ridiculous notions that 'good mom's' deliver babies "naturally." It is not somehow more natural to face the most painful experience you will ever experience in your entire life with absolutely no pain relief. Would men do this??

When you have a headache you take an aspirin, it's not "un-natural." In fact aspirin was discovered because people were eating plants and herbs trying to cope with pain and painful medical treatments and discovered that chewing on willow bark sure did help. Was that 'un-natural?' Can you picture them saying, "oh the pain!... no - no medicine man - no bark for me - I want to be in pain naturally."

If you feel like pain will be an important part of your birth experience then I understand. Truly I do. I don't run marathons - but I get that some people find a lot of meaning from them - and if experiencing the full brunt of the pain is valuable to you then - truly - that is awesome. But try not to parade your decision to suffer the experience - as though it was a merit badge. At the end of the experience the woman in horrible pain and the woman with the epidural both have a baby... and that was the point wasn't it??

And if you did forgo anesthesia please don't tell everyone that it wasn't so bad. There are two types of women who say that childbirth -"wasn't so bad." Women with big awesome birthing hips who really didn't rip their vagina from stem to stern in delivery, and evil, self-important, punks who are trying to ruin everything for the rest of us.

Seriously.

If you had little pain during your delivery quit prancing around telling the rest of the world about your amazing "natural" delivery as though those of us who got some drugs somehow had 'synthetic deliveries.' As though we are lesser woman then you for admitting that it hurt like hell.

Sure, maybe you have the Zen like self-control of a Tibetan Buddhist who can control his body temperature with his thoughts... or maybe you have a huge vag... really.

Or maybe you just like being pretentious and condescending.

Either way it's not going to win you a ton of friends with those of us who were torn apart to our hind ends and are just thrilled that we can poop normally because it was touch and go there for a few days.

By the way, another friend of mine (who is a Dentist) donates time giving free dental care to folks in third world countries who regularly do have their dental care performed 'naturally,' and you know what?? They stinking LOVE anesthesia!

NOW WHAT?

When my friend got pregnant at 20 she had only been married for a couple of months and was not at all prepared for motherhood. I remember talking with her on the phone in her last trimester and she kept saying that she couldn't imagine what was going to happen after delivering. She felt like she would have the big dramatic day of delivery and then.... it would just be done.

Tada! You're not pregnant!

But she could not imagine what came after that??

I always felt the same way - what on earth comes next? Well - here you go.

What comes next?

First of all - sleeplessness.

And the best trick to help with that? Attachment parenting... kind of...

I never did attachment parenting officially - but I

think it's awesome! The actress from Blossom and the Big Bang Theory, Mayam Balik, is a big advocate and she's written a book on it. And although I never officially intended to do attachment parenting, and there are some elements of it that I didn't do at all, I would say I came pretty close on my own.

We never let our babies sleep in the hospital nursery without us. I breast fed exclusively and did not allow a baby bottle in the house for several months so as to avoid there being any option other than breastfeeding. I did sleep with my oldest in a separate room for the first couple of weeks. But I quickly decided that it was a mistake.

He had colic and screamed from about 4 pm until 4 am for weeks. It was horrible. But I did realize with my subsequent children that they seemed to sleep so much better just sleeping right next to me. There are awesome side beds that fit onto your own bed so that you can slide your baby back and forth for breast feeding and that way you don't run the risk of them getting rolled on or slipping between a mattress and wall. It is SO wonderful. You will not believe how much better you sleep as a mom when you don't actually have to wake up for breast-feeding during the night. You just wake up enough to help her latch on and then when she's done at some point, you slide her back to the side sleeper.

Here's my very best bit of advice to a first time

mom, and if I could wave a magic wand and make this possible for every family on earth I would.

Just stop. Everything.

If it's not about you and your new baby don't bother with it. I would strongly, strongly encourage every woman to just stop, for a couple of months, if at all possible.

Don't worry about food or laundry or work. Nothing. These first few weeks are so physically draining and yet there are moments of absolute magic and any effort you make toward anything but sleep and snuggling is an absolute waste.

You need rest. Desperately. Let people come and visit the baby now and then, but have your husband stick a note on the door that you are sleeping and not to be disturbed whenever you can.

Sleep all day when the baby is sleeping and be up at night with him when he's up. It's so much easier than trying to fight it. You both will have your days and nights fixed up soon enough.

If it's possible - get him out into the sunshine during the day when he is awake. But when he's napping - go and nap. Keep the ice on your hoo-ha and waddle around your apartment in nothing but jammies for weeks. Don't feel any pressure from anyone to wear yourself out, or to miss out on the sleeping and cuddling. It's such a physically, mentally and spiritually demanding time. And I really believe that it is a time that we as women should absolutely demand that the world back the heck off and let it be about Mom and Baby sleeping and recovering from trauma and starting the family bonding.

Just this one time in your whole entire life: Demand something. This is such an important time and it is too important to miss out on it. To be stressed out is such a waste. In a few short weeks your baby will only be up a couple of times during the night and will just feed and go right back to sleep.

In a few more weeks he will start crawling and playing. A few weeks after that he won't have to breast feed every two hours but just a few times a day. This is a very short, very magical time.

You will be exhausted and sore, your boobs will be exploding and you may have depression as hormones purge from your system. Don't fall into the trap that our modern world has laid for women.

Don't allow some episode of Friends or some Glamor magazine with an actress who's out flashing rock hard abs ten days after her baby was born pressure you. She has a nanny and millions of dollars and to be honest I don't envy her - at all. I bet she wishes that she could just cuddle and rest instead of feeling the pressure to show off.

BREASTFEEDING

So you got through the discomfort of childbirth and pregnancy and now you're done. Time to just chill out and relax - right? Wrong. Your boobies are about to triple in size.

And then they are going to go absolutely nuts. I can't even begin to explain the chaos that will be going on right under your chin. And I mean right under your chin. When your milk comes in those suckers will be sitting up that stinking high. They grow by the second. And if you feed the baby on one it will shrink up a bit. So you can actually squeeze your boobs and tell which one was used last.

Do you remember that Austin Power's movie where the Barbie robots shot bullets out of their ta-tas?? You will be that robot. (That wasn't really all that funny was it? I know men were laughing but I just thought it was awkward.) Well - this will be even more awkward. Milk - real honest to goodness milk - will shoot out of your BODY!!

Imagine if it was coming out of your elbow? It's bizarre. You are a real person - a normal functioning person, but for a few years of your life you will be a person who produces milk. It'll just be something you do.

And for a while it won't just come out when beckoned - it will be shooting out... all the time. You will fill up pads full of milk. At the most awkward and inappropriate times a big wet splotch will start growing on your top. And this isn't the worst of it.

There was something that no one probably told you. Breastfeeding really, really, hurts at the beginning.

I don't know why it is that no one tells you this. Maybe because it's just too much. I remember when I was in my first pregnancy, at about my sixth month, and I was still vomiting constantly, that was when my mother decided to explain to me how painful breastfeeding actually is.

I freaked out.

I couldn't imagine how I was going to get through another day of vomiting and she was telling me that this was going to get super painful... after the whole childbirth stuff? So - I guess I can understand not wanting to overwhelm women - it's kind-of like when you discuss childbirth. You don't want to freak people out after all - so you downplay it - until you're in a room full of women who've had kids, then you go nuts with the horrific details.

So the first few times the baby latches on aren't too rough - but once your milk comes in it gets very, very, painful.

This is one reason that I am really glad that I didn't have any bottles around. It really does get better, and the week or so of pain is pretty quick compared to nausea or healing your nether region. Day by day the pain subsides. But the first few days after your milk lets down are just awful.

I hope you'll stick it out if it is possible. Breastfeeding is such a beautiful precious experience and I really think it helps with postpartum. I have never met a woman who did breastfeed and regretted it.

If you haven't already had this data shoved at you then allow me to be the first of many - If you have read these stats a million times... well sorry.

Stats for Breastfeeding

(This section I stole from ask.com directly.)

1. Increases Baby's IQ

Breastfeeding has been shown to increase your baby's intelligence quotient (IQ). The average increase is about 7 points. While it might not be the difference for acceptance to Harvard, we all need every point we can get!

2. Helps mom lose that baby fat.

There are certain fat stores that go on your body during pregnancy that are destined to be for breastfeeding. Breastfeeding helps tap into those stores and reduce the fat deposits laid down in pregnancy.

3. Breastfed babies are less likely to die of SIDS.

About 7,000 US babies die every year from SIDS. While we don't know what causes SIDS, we do know what the risk factors are, that includes using formula to feed your baby. Breast milk is one of the few factors that you can control.

4. Reduced allergies for breastfed babies.

Breastfeeding your baby causes baby to have fewer allergies. There are lots of reasons why this happens, but remember - Mother's milk is specific for each and every child. It changes throughout the day and throughout the span that you nurse.

5. The American Academy of Pediatrics (AAP) recommends that your baby begin breastfeeding within the first hour of life and that they only receive breast milk until they are older. It's also recommended by the American Dietetic Association (ADA), the World Health Organization (WHO) and UNICEF.

6. Breastfeeding burns calories!

Breastfeeding requires about 500 calories a day to simply produce the milk. You can use those extra 500 calories to add more food to your diet or to help you lose weight after the birth.

7. Formula increases the risk of diabetes (type I).

Infants who are exposed to formula, particularly early on have a greater likelihood to develop Type I diabetes. Infants who were expressly breastfed for at least 5 months with no formula had lower rates of Type I diabetes. The longer they were breastfed, the lower the risk.

8. Post-birth benefits are also many.

By breastfeeding your body releases a hormone that helps your uterus contract, oxytocin. This can reduce your risk of postpartum hemorrhage or the need for other medications. Nursing also helps your uterus heal after birth and get back to its pre-pregnancy size.

9. Cancers decrease with breastfeeding too.

Your risk of developing breast cancer and other cancers is increased if you do not breast feed. Breastfeeding can help lower the incidence of breast cancer, ovarian cancer, endometrial cancer, etc.

10. Breastfeeding lowers the risk of obesity.

Not only will breastfeeding make your child leaner and healthy, it will help reduce days missed at work for illnesses, etc. Because nursing lowers the risk that your child will suffer from upper respiratory infections, ear infections, etc.

So yeah, the statistics to support breastfeeding are really strong, but - if you hate it, or can't make it work - give yourself a break. Plenty of healthy, happy, wonderful, people were never breastfed and are plugging along just fine. Life is not a one size fits all proposition.

While I admit that I am pretty friggin' ingenious,

I'm not you and just because I think something is awesome doesn't mean I know what's best for you and your life. Is breastfeeding best for your baby - yes. The stats are clear. But is it best for you and your baby?? I can't know that. Being the best Mom you can be requires difficult choices - and unfortunately this is not the most difficult.

LIFE ONE-HANDED

Another new development after this baby is born? How to do anything and everything one handed. I mean everything. You will change diapers with one hand. Pull out a stroller and get it open and loaded with one hand. Cook dinner, wash dishes, fold laundry. Everything. One hand... and sometimes a little help from your mouth. You think I'm making a big deal out of nothing? Let's put you into a scenario you are sure to encounter...

Target. "Ahhhhh!" (Say the 'Ahhh' part like a chorus of angels...) Try it again.

Target... "Ahhhh!"

That amazing world where you walk in for toilet paper and walk out with $200 worth of stuff that you had no idea you needed. It's a spell, a wicked spell is cast upon you before you have even made it past the parking lot....

"Look at those lovely switch plate covers! They would look so pretty in the kitchen. I should get those, they would increase my home's value - so I'm actually investing - not spending. If I'm getting some for the kitchen maybe for the bedroom?? Kid's room? Of course, my daughter won't like the lovely one with the rose buds... she'll want the Dora one..."

And while my brain is distracted by the money that I'm soon to be arguing to my husband was a reasonable and important investment, all the while begging him to help me get them screwed into the old switch plate (because who knew the screws would be in that tight? - seriously?)- the baby is starting to pull stuff off the shelf and I realize that I have to pee...

Dum-dum-dah!!... (sing that with the 'scary music sound' in your head... do you know what I mean here?? The sound that tells you something important and kinda bad has just been revealed??)

Why?? Why, you ask, is this a big deal? I just have to go pee... with a baby....

I have done this so many times now that I could do it in my sleep - but the first time you do it... it's more difficult than anything.

You have never seen difficult!!!

Complex physics problems- involving every freaking letter of the alphabet and some imaginary numbers (whatever the heck those things even are) and sequencing and a few 'square root of blah blah whatevers,' thrown in... All of that - it has nothing on going to the bathroom with a baby who is NOT in a car seat.

Why is she not in the car seat? Because you were

just coming in for a package of toilet paper. Remember? And plus - she hates the car seat! Hates it!

Because, you didn't give birth to one of those adorable, smiley, little, patient babies like that annoying friend of yours who never has stains on her shirt... No, you gave birth to a future 'Circe-du-Sole' acrobat who treats a car seat as the most extreme punishment ever invented.

On the plus side, discipline is a piece of cake... torturing her is as simple as a car ride, in the car seat - (facing backwards for safety of course). The downside is convincing her that she deserves to be punished several times a day so you can run errands.

And is she strapped into the front of the cart? Maybe - because if she can chew on the shopping cart handle for a while that seems to keep her entertained. (Don't judge me - it is good for her immune system, I have decided.) When you cover that handle with that anti-bacterial gunk do you know what you've done? You have killed off 99% of the bacteria that was festering on that handle.

That means you left 1%. What do you suppose that 1% remaining is??

And are you that Mom that wraps the whole thing in a fabric whatjamajob? Way to try to make the rest of us feel bad - but here's the truth.

The fabric thingy gets covered in the bacteria - and then you throw it on the couch or floor or whatever and the baby shoves that in her mouth - or you touch the fabric thing with your hands and then the germs are on your hands and then your baby shoves your hand into her mouth.

Here's the deal - for whatever reason 90% of the germs on the planet will be shoved into your beautiful, precious, innocent, baby girl in that first year because she is going to shove every stinking thing into her mouth and the more you wash your hands and sanitize the heck out of stuff the more likely that the only stuff she is actually managing to get exposed to is the super deadly anti-bacterial resistant stuff, and then she has too few good critters running around in her body to fight off those gnarly germs with.

So as for me?? My baby girl is going to be chewing and drooling all over that shopping cart handle and I'm not going to bat an eye.

(By the way, nothing I say here should be taken as medical advice, and I have absolutely no actual evidence for any of my opinions and following my example should be assumed to be a rather stupid and illogical choice and should not be done under any circumstances.)

But... is my daughter strapped safely in the front of the cart chewing on the handle?? Probably not. She is probably in the main basket crawling around with a toy that I snagged from the toy section, which I have every intention of leaving on some random shelf right before I get to the checkout stand. (Hey

Target store, you just talked me into spending $200 when I came in with the intention of only spending $10 so let's agree that you can put the light up Dora toy away when I leave it somewhere totally inappropriate. We still are not even.)

And can you bring the shopping cart into the bathroom? No! Because all those stinking thieves have ruined that option for the rest of us. Using their kids to smuggle stuff out of grocery stores, so no way would they allow you to bring the cart in the bathroom now.

So you park your cart in the lineup of carts near the bathroom and head in with the child tucked onto your left hip. And I want you to pause and think about what happens next...

This is a crawling baby. This is a baby somewhere between, say, 5 months and a year and a half. This baby is in love with the ground.

She wants to be on it constantly. She loves to roll around on it, mouth wide open - tongue lolling out as she shoves anything and everything she can get her hands on into her mouth. And for all my shopping cart handle chew-toy belief system - even I would never ever set a crawling baby on the floor of a public bathroom.

So are you starting to see your problem here?? Baby - bathroom- floor.... And now you see where the difficulty level goes up.

Maybe you have a chill baby and there is that

changing table in the handicapped bathroom - and maybe (even though it says not to) you plop you baby on it and strap them in and then pee as fast as possible while watching them squiggle around... inches from death. Maybe you're a horrible parent like that.

But maybe you're not a terrible person, or maybe you too are raising a baby who finds that 'straps' are obstacles meant to be overcome as she begins her steady march toward world domination - so you know that nothing on earth could be as dumb as putting your baby in a precarious location with nothing more substantive holding her down than a flimsy strap.

So here we are... this is happening.

You are wearing a belt. (Just for added difficulty...)

Baby on the left hip - You must now, with only your right hand available, unfasten your belt, and unbutton your jeans... Did you make it this far one handed?? Now we have to undo the zipper.

Yeah!! - maybe if you kinda spread your feet apart you can get some tension on the zipper?? Help you out a bit??

You know what? Forget it. Let's just start pulling the jeans down and the zipper will give with all the wiggling. All right hike your left arm with the baby up on your rib - lean to the right and give the jeans on your left a big tug with your right hand. There you go - now the right side. Back to the left. The back the right... And finally success - you are completely disrobed down to your knees with a fully alive baby in your left arm and a third of your shirt in her mouth.

Plop down on the toilet, detangle your shirt from her fist, and bounce her on one knee as you finish your business. Now...

Now we gotta get all of this back up again don't we?

Up you go... wiggle wiggle - spread your feet for friction - bounce. Don't drop the baby - she's got your necklace. Pull, cuss, pull, cry, shift, swear you are going to lose another five pounds. There!!

The jeans are up and the baby is alive - thank God for auto flush toilets... But your zipper, button.... your belt. And only one hand!!

No getting out of it - you can do this. And you know what? You really can - I've done it so many gazzilions of times! Hook your finger through the buttonhole, grab the button and, about twenty minutes later, you'll have it buttoned! Don't bother with the zipper - just get that snuck in from behind the shopping cart. But the belt? Why were we wearing a belt? Oh, you can't leave for the cart with that undone! One handed - thread it through - hold the baby off to the side like a football - bite your lower lip - poke and poke and poke that darn metal jobby at the belt until the miracle occurs and you have gotten it through!! Nice!

Head up! Open the door and face the sink. Ignore the odd looks from other women at all the fiasco they have been listening to. Time to wash your hands. One at a time. Right first - wash, rinse - switch baby to right - wash left - towel and exit!!!! Yes!!! You did it!!

Don't forget to zip you pants!

BODY BACK AFTER BABY

This article was reprinted with permission from SanJuan-parent.com. It is the first article in a 4 part series on tips I have for getting your figure back after pregnancy. If you are interested in my tips please check out my subsequent posts there.

First of all, I need to admit that I am not – NOT – a supermodel look-a-like. If you saw me walking down the street your first thought would not be "How does she look so good?" It wouldn't be your fifth thought. It wouldn't be a thought that you would ever have.

But, I have been in a long drawn out war with my body – trying to keep it decent enough to wear a bikini since I had my son over a decade ago. And while I haven't exactly succeeded, I wear the bikini anyway. I do know many Moms who have kept their figure's far better than I, but I have put myself through several different experiments trying to find ways to support my irrational vanity in the face of mother nature and I know some of them are rather unusual, and they did seem to help. So, while I may not look, at all, like a supermodel – I do look a whole lot better than I would have otherwise. So, over the next few months I'll share my favorite tips – and some that totally failed. Hope you find something you like.

Now, I know most every single pregnancy magazine article about recovering your figure begins with a lesson in being healthy before you even get pregnant and eating healthy throughout. So I will devote all of one sentence to the idea: Don't live on soda and chips and cookies and expect that you will look gorgeous; maybe you could do that at 22 but you can't at 32 and the sooner you start living on salads and yogurt the better you will look.

Reality: I had ZERO control over what I ate when I was pregnant. I am normally pretty healthy – but I was sick as a dog throughout my pregnancies. I lost weight for the first 6 months – then I gained tons of weight till the end. My ability to choose what was going in my stomach was nil. Most everything that went down was coming back up and I made food choices based on which foods 'throw up' best. So by the time my kids were born I was around 40 lbs. over my starting weight. A little more than necessary, but not too bad – (although as short as I am I think I could have gained only 25…)

Now, assuming you had one of those pregnancies where you could control what you ate and could do some moderate exercise – great. But wherever you are today is where you are, and instead of wasting time discussing how you should have eaten before you were pregnant, I want to discuss something else you should have done before you got pregnant.

Don't date a jerk. Seriously.

The truth is you are NEVER EVER going to truly "get your body back after baby." Not really. You can pay a plastic surgeon tons, you can use every trick in the book and you can get pretty dang hot, but you will never be as hot as you would have been if you hadn't had the baby in the first place.

You are sacrificing some of your looks for the sake of your child. Get used to it. You are going to sacrifice a whole lot more than that for this kid. And they are worth it.

But, if you're with some jerk who wants you to be his 20 year old fantasy female you are going to have a long miserable life. If you divorce him and try to find someone else you are likely to wind up with another jerk, because we have all noticed that women tend to habitually pick the same 'quality' of men over and over. If you have been dating jerks you need to figure out what you're doing, and why you're doing it. It's important. You shouldn't be in a relationship with a jerk. You really shouldn't be raising a kid with a jerk. And you really really shouldn't be raising a kid when you have issues that make you want love from jerks.

Find a good man who loves you because you are his best friend. If he just loves being with a 'sexy woman' he is going to be pretty miserable with a woman who is 'post baby' with milk shooting out of her boobs, a belly that looks like a deflated balloon and who hasn't slept more than two hours at a time for weeks on end.

Find the guy who will rise to that occasion and would love you for the mother you are, for the sacrifices you are making, for the strength you demonstrate. So, I know telling you this now is of no help to you, you already made a baby with the guy you made a baby with, but it's the truth – so pass it on to the unmarried women in your life. We need to stop wasting time with men who aren't going to be good fathers.

The other truth is – (and this is a hard one to admit) people live up to (and down to) what we will accept. If you are accepting that a man's value of you can be based on nothing more than your appearance, then don't be surprised if it is. If you expect that a man loves your heart, your character and mind far more than your body – then he will live up to that, and you won't be attracted to any man who doesn't.

There are women far far uglier than you who

have men who are terribly in love with them, and there are women far, far more beautiful than you who cannot find a man who will love them and remain faithful to them (think Hollywood).

Beauty has ALMOST NOTHING to do with whether or not you marry a good man, a good father, and a good husband. That has EVERYTHING to do with your own beliefs about what you deserve in life.

So the very first step in getting your "body back after baby" is accepting that – you won't.

BREASTFEEDING BLOG

Here's an idea! Someone needs to start a blog called 'weird places I've had to breastfeed.' Maybe someone has?

Wait!!

Please submit to me, all necessary rights and perpetuities and whatnot.

There! I'm certain that that was legally binding. But if you are planning to start that website – (and thanks in advance for the check!!) I think I could add a few stories to your page.

Weird places that I have managed to breast feed...?

Well, I have on countless occasions breastfed at restaurants. This is not so bad actually because you're sitting and the tablecloth kind of hides some of the boob exposure. It's actually a really nice place for public feeding. Except that my kids did not like it when they couldn't see. So they would immediately start pulling at the pretty blanket I would toss over us for modesty. I would often finagle it so it was modest enough, but they could still see out somewhere. And we would be going along just fine, and then (this would always seem to happen just as I was in the middle of a fascinating conversation about really important stuff):

"Yes, I do think that the Middle East oil crisis could be mitigated with a substantial investment in..."

Just at this point in my fascinating and poignant observation a little hand would shoot up and throw the blanket off of my chest exposing the baby with her mouth full of... well me...

It was kind of a conversation killer.

Some other awkward moments...?

There was the time we decided to carpool with some friends and (do you remember how I mention that my baby's HATE car seats and HATE facing backwards in their car seats?? I'm pretty confident they lost IQ points being stuck in that place. But, you know, safety first etc.

So there we are - in a car, with our friends - and our baby is screaming. There's a solution here. I can feed the baby. But of course we are not pulling the baby out of the car seat... we aren't barbarians.

So, there was a conversation. I apologize for the noise. We try pacifiers and toys, but eventually my husband and I mention that if we were alone in the car there is something we would do... Our friends show interest. They make it clear they are much more interested in stopping the screaming than in protecting my modesty. So, I did the reasonable thing. I un-buckled, leaned my body over the car seat, undid my top... no biggie.

It wasn't uncomfortable - at all... And our friends don't still tell that story to this day.

Another awkward time:

We were riding in a car with some friends and the baby was screaming....

Yeah - I've done this to more than one set of friends...

But, probably the most awkward was at a hot springs. I live in a rural part of... The United States of America - and near where I live there may or may not be some hot-springs.

(Why are you so interested in where I live?? Are you with the NSA?? Get off of me!)

I am NOT a naked hippy-dip kind of girl. No matter how hard my husband has tried. Exhibition-ism-ness is NOT in my blood.

But a public hot-springs pool in mid-winter is actually a pretty private place. The fog coming off of the water is so thick that someone has to be within about two feet to see you.

So there we are - the whole family - and we're floating around the pool and the baby is getting fussy.

Now, I need you to picture the circumstances

properly. It's night. It's freezing - mid winter - the water on the side of the pool is ice. And it's super foggy so you really can't see a bit. And of course I'm not going to try to pull a towel or something into the pool to cover up with. I'd drown the poor kiddo - but there's no way I'm getting out of the pool and into the freezing air until the very second we leave.

So, I head over to a corner of the pool and my husband is splashing around with big brother a few feet away as I pop my ta-ta out of my bathing suit in this private little space.

Instantly some ratty old hippie dude decides to show up and have a conversation with me about his love for children and the importance of breastfeeding.

Never ever saw him coming.

He moved through the fog like a little water bug and was in my face before I knew what hit me. And of course my husband has no clue since it's so foggy and night. He just thinks his chatty wife is annoying some poor local fella with her constant chatter, no idea that, for once, this conversation involves me as the victim.

I'm too scared to pull my baby off, and since I'd gone to a private little corner to do this I am now literally cornered. The "conversation," lasted for a bit before my husband caught on. If you thought I was uncomfortable alone, you should have felt the vibe when my husband joined the club. The two of us just staring at our new friend who is chatting away while the baby just enjoys her dinner. Trying to get him to catch on and leave us was futile. He is still here right now... staring at me as I type this. He really can't seem to take a hint.

SEX AFTER BABY

You know what you will be thinking in the last few pushes before the baby arrives?? (Or if you're epiduraled up – the thought may not hit you until the numbness wears off.)

This is what you will be thinking: "Nothing – certainly not that man I married – is ever EVER going anywhere near my va-jay-jay EVER AGAIN!!

This is a thought that won't go away. (No I'm not talking to you Ms. "I loved childbirth/ what tearing? /I had an ethereal out of body orgasmic experience when I delivered.") We all hate you… ok- we might not hate you, but we resent that you are not miserable… quite a bit – and we might be jealous.

So for all of us who tear and bleed profusely and spend the next month with frozen maxi pads in our crotches – this is the thinking. Things got destroyed down yonder and we are leaving that land fallow – for – like ever.

And I know you want me to tell you that it magically goes away. That you wake up one morning and you are healed and whole and the man who created this beautiful life with you is by your side and you fall into an embrace of such great love and passion the world has never known.

This is NOT what happens. What happens is a man who has patiently gone through your nasty, barfy, lazy, first trimester – and then through your get away from me 'it hurts to sit' last trimester – has now been asked to go through 6 weeks of zero physical contact. And there is this doctor's appointment where he is going to be given the ok to share all the love that has been building up inside of him. (Love – that is what has been building… love.)

I know what you are hoping. You are hoping that at that appointment the doctor will say, "Oh – heck no!! She is not ready for any such naughtiness young man!! You back off and leave her alone!" But that is not what the doctor will say; he will say, "Yep, good to go!" And you will be very tempted to pull your foot out of the stirrup and kick him in the teeth.

Really! What does he know?

I (and this is not medical advice – this was probably a very stupid idea… that I had – with every single pregnancy) did not eat solid food for a while after the baby was born. Not in the first few days. But about a week after they were born and I'd had a few poops that made me want to die – I decided to just quit eating anything solid.

I lived on juice smoothies with yogurt. I just needed a break from pooping to heal. I know - this is gross, but how many gross things have I already confessed at this point? – We should just assume I have zero shame left now.

Am I saying anyone should do this? Nope. In fact I can hear wise OBGYN's in my head right now saying that I should have been eating high fiber whatnots and vegetables.

But it was my hoo-ha that was blown out and I was not interested in doing any pushing that wasn't caused by a sneeze. And, by the way, totally worth it! I made it a good week or so without a BM and the chance to heal made my life much better.

So when six week mark rolls around and the all-knowing doctor or midwife has confirmed that in his or her mind you are totally ready to have an invasion into the land recently desolated by nuclear holocaust- here's how you do it.

Wine. I'd say a couple of glasses. Don't forget to express some milk afterwards – we don't want intoxicated newborns. Then, we need a sweet moment with the man you love. You hold his hands – look deep into his eyes, and you tell him that if he starts banging around down there you are going to make him suffer like he has never, ever, known. In a sweet voice – of course.

Then you might want to put a pillow over your head, because, for some reason, men enjoy knowing that we enjoy their lovemaking… and you are probably not going to enjoy this. This is going to be a celebration in which you will not be partaking in the festivities, so if you want to hide your grimaces and such it might be a good idea.

If and when it hurts you just let him know, and between the two of you make a night of it. I know you may feel like holding out on him indefinitely – for several years at least. But, it is important to remember what an intense and loving experience you have shared, and that he has been looking at you as you love his child and feeling so close to you and proud of you and he really is ready for that connection.

It is important to maintain the closeness and bond that is growing between you, because there are also those nights when you are screaming at one another that the baby is too cold, or needs to be fed or put to bed to 'cry it out,' and you don't agree and can't stop fighting and kinda hate each other.

So the bond and love that has been growing through this process really needs to be nurtured and cultivated. You both really do need this. He needs to hold the woman he loves – and he's obsessed with your gigantic boobs too.

MOTHERHOOD

Let's boil it down for a second, the good, the bad, the ugly... the awesome:

The good - well of course this is the moments cuddling your baby, the first time you see your husband plant a kiss on that little forehead. Waking up in the morning with that tiny body snuggled up next to you.

The bad - Oh man. There are some rough days. You kid throwing a tantrum in the store while you get angry stares. The messes that never ever end. Watching your husband twitch as he drives down the road with a screaming baby- mine once said that he didn't know why the FBI didn't just use a screaming baby to torture people.

The ugly... do yourself a favor - don't under any circumstances get a look at your naked body for six months... no eight months... at least a year. Wait a really long time before you take a real look.

And the awesome:

The feeling of a tiny hand wrapped tight around your finger. Even better, the first time your baby's hands wrap around your neck, or the first time you hear the words: "I lob you mom." And you know what - my oldest is closing in on tweenager-hood and I still, to this day, get a small thrill every time he tells me he loves me. It's just worth every single sacrifice.

HOW YOUR MARRIAGE WILL CHANGE

Every couple has to renegotiate their relationship after a baby comes into the picture. In fact - if you think about it, the changes have likely already begun. Pregnancy alone tends to make the relationship shift a bit. It's likely the first time you have really had to lean on your husband, and the first time he has felt that helplessness that comes from watching someone he loves struggle with things that he truly cannot change.

This is probably good, because if you haven't yet noticed, men seem to have an intense need to treat every issue as though it is a flat tire that can just be patched and thrown back on the rim. It's hard to clarify that sometimes the only solution is just to be present. Pregnancy is FULL of times in which all he will be able to do is be present.

Every couple I know had a difficult time negotiating this transition into living with this new member of the family. Imagine, for a minute, how your marriage would handle it if his best friend moved in with the two of you. What about if it was your best friend? There really isn't anyone who could move into your home without it doing some damage to the two of you, right?? And, those were your best friends! People who are in your life because you love them by choice.

This baby is not your best friend. This is someone who is downright needy. They are impossible to communicate with, and they ONLY complain.

Think about that for a minute.

A newborn cannot communicate gratitude. They can't tell you that they appreciate eating, or the home, or the clothes, or the cute little nursery. All the effort you've put into creating them, birthing them, and providing for them, and the ONLY communication they have is crying. They let you know when they are unhappy with life, and never ever tell you that they are pleased.

I remember talking with my girlfriends after we had our babies and all of us had a few big fights with our husbands in the weeks after we brought our first baby home. I think part of the fighting comes from just being so dang tired that you literally find yourself waking up in weird places. But, it also comes from the desperate concern you suddenly feel for your new baby.

My husband and I have had countless arguments over choices we were making about our baby. What lotion we could use, what laundry soap, how tight the straps on the car seat should be. We both felt strongly about our opinions and we weren't arguing about something simple, it was our child. The most precious thing on the entire planet to us, and how do you compromise when caring for this baby is so dang important?

You want to know the most bizarre moment that you will face? It will come when you are having an argument about something... Let's say you want to start giving the baby a couple of bites of baby cereal in the evening. But your husband thinks it's too early for the baby to start getting solids of any kind. You say your mother was giving you baby cereal when you were only a few weeks old, and you made it, and your baby is much older than that. He points to some statistics showing higher allergies and obesity rates for kids who get cereal too early. You think that's convenient for him because he doesn't have to be up feeding a baby all night. This fight is a fierce one. Lines have been drawn and neither of you has any intention of backing down... and then he does it...

He picks up the baby and walks out into the back yard....

It is ridiculous... you know it's no big deal. But you are ready to head to the phone and call the cops and tell them that your husband has abducted your child.

Yep. That's a whole new level of crazy. But it's your baby. It's your everything. You would die in a heartbeat before you would ever, ever let something happen to your baby and he just took him!! Just took him and walked out the door...

I promise, if you think I'm crazy I'm really not... this will twist your brain into a knot and it will take every ounce of self-control you have to set your phone down and refrain from having him thrown in the slammer!! (That's what they're calling it these days right?)

Another thing that may happen to you? You may just resent the hell out of your husband - for.... well.... for being a man really.

Because at the end of the day, the Mom is the Mom. You have the boobies - you most likely will be doing the lion's share of the feeding. And even if you are a working mom and he is a stay at home dad and he does all the housework and feedings, you will likely resent him for that too.

Becoming a Mom, regardless of how it works out for your family, means you will recognize certain sacrifices that you are making that your husband is not. If you do have to work you will probably resent that you have to. You will miss being with your baby - there will be guilt when you can't see their first steps, be there when they are hurt or lonely, and the things you will miss, from field trips to Christmas performances will only get worse as they get older.

If you do stay home, you will resent missing out on the rest of the world. You will miss having a career, and using your brain. You will wonder who you are independent of diapers and cleaning.

And no matter what you do, one night you will be up at 3 am. Bleary eyed and frustrated and you will go into the bedroom where your husband is snoring away in total peace and contentment and you will punch him in the face.

You think I'm joking?

I had a friend who totally admitted to doing this. I will never ever reveal my source, but I swear to you she is a wonderful woman - she just snapped.

You may not punch your sleeping husband in the face, but I bet you will do what most of us have... you will yell at him.

I bet there will be a night where you are so tired, and feel so lost - that the sight of him still just being himself, while you feel like your whole world was thrown up in the air and landed in a huge mess, will make you flip your lid. And you will feel compelled to wake him up and make sure he suffers a bit for having put you here.

Of course, it isn't rational, and of course his life has been affected too. Of course he needs his sleep too - and he's struggling with the changes too. But the odds are pretty good, that at some point that disparity I mentioned with the whole "Adam and Eve thing," will just hit the boiling point and you will have to let it out - at 3 am - when he's fast asleep.

But, hey, when he's screaming at you that you are bat-%*&#&$* crazy and he did nothing to deserve getting woken up and yelled at - just let him know that you were exercising restraint and not all husbands have been so lucky. (Don't punch your husband in the face - seriously - it's kind of funny, but it's wrong. I shouldn't have to tell you this, you're a grown woman and you know this, but seriously. You can't punch people, it's called assault - you will go to jail.)

COLIC

If you're baby winds up having colic I just want to let you know how very sorry I am. Our firstborn had colic and I really would have said that after all we had been through with pregnancy, everything else in life would be a cakewalk. But no... No it wasn't.

Colic for those of you unfamiliar - is a completely unknown "condition" in which you baby cries for hours on end, for no discernible reason. I'd like to tell you why they are crying, but so far the medical community has very little to say about the entire subject.

Have you noticed a theme with the medical community?? Why am I throwing up? Why am I spitting, why does childbirth hurt, why is my baby crying?? The answer is the same... "We don't really know why it is that blah -blah -blah..."

Hey, I'm sure they wish they knew so they could

give us a pill and get us to leave them alone. I think that actually the answer is so much worse than any of us want to hear. The truth??

The truth is that life just really sucks - a lot of the time - and that it sucks when everything is just fine.

Horrible, smash your head against the side of the car door childbirth?? That's perfectly normal and healthy. Non-stop vomiting in early pregnancy - that's good, just as it should be. Colicky baby? Not ideal - not every baby has it, but nothing is wrong. Some babies just scream from 4 pm until 4 am every single day for weeks. And there's nothing - wrong - with - that. Excellent.

One of the first nights after we brought that first baby home, I remember being up in the middle of the night with him just screaming his little head off. I was trying to change his diaper thinking maybe it would help and he peed on me. I was in my bed (which was already starting to smell like sour milk) and now it had pee on it too... and, of course, I was still bleeding.

It hit me all at once - the overwhelming amount of fluids. Pee, blood, milk, tears... then I started crying - and my milk let down - and he spit up. More fluids. Weird body fluids everywhere. All over my bed, my clothes, my home.

My husband found us like that when he came in to see what was going on. Me cross-legged on the bed bawling with the baby on my lap screaming and wet damp jammies and sheets and mess. It was a breakdown of epic proportions.

I have that moment burned in my memory. So dang tired, so filthy, so overwhelmed. I don't remember how it ended. I don't remember getting the little troublemaker to sleep or cleaning the bed up. I just remember the misery of that moment.

If you are feeling really sorry for me, and of course you should - I have to admit that I have another image burned into my mind as well.

It is of my husband. He is sitting in a rocking chair with our firstborn in his arms, and he has found some ear plugs (not the little orange jobbies that you shove into your ears, but those big padded deals that you use at a shooting range or around airplanes) - because the scrawny brand new baby in his arms is screaming at the top of his lungs.

My husband is staring straight ahead, and he doesn't so much as blink when I walk into the room. He just stares straight ahead and keeps rocking. It was one of the greatest acts of mental focus I have seen him endure.

This man is an amazing athlete - he, of his own free will, requires stitches and casts very regularly. He loves sports that involve a highly unnecessary amount of risk, and suffering. I don't know why he is wired this way. I try to avoid pain and suffering as a matter of daily practice. But for my husband it's addictive... pain... yummy! But, this man who loves to suffer was using every ounce of mental focus he could muster in order to sit and rock the screaming baby.

Here's what I can tell you parents that are suffering colic - it DOES get better. It is so awful - but it is only for a short time. You know how the screaming always seems to kick in at the same time and last for about the same amount of time? That window of screaming will just get shorter and shorter and within a few weeks it will be over. Until then, get earplugs. That's all I got for you. Earplugs.

TIME TO PUT ON YOUR BIG GIRL PANTIES

Priorities

I have made a list of career goals now that my kids are getting older and I recognize that I am ready to start working outside the home more. Here they are:

1. Make sure I am always making my kids my number one priority. No matter what else comes up in life, being the very best mother I can possibly be is always my highest priority. And if my child needs me to, I will sacrifice any career goals, any personal ambition, and personal desire in order to ensure that they grow into kind, good, healthy, courageous, compassionate, people who will work hard to make this world a better place.

1. Don't screw up goal #1.

1. Seriously.

1. Start working on writing more and see if you're able to actually get paid.

There. Those are my life goals right now. I should add that a huge part of goal #1 is working on my marriage, because if I can't ensure my kids have a strong relationship with a loving Dad then I have already hurt goal #1.

THE IMPORTANCE OF DADS

Dads are the primary source of a person's self-esteem in my completely unscientific opinion. If you don't have a Dad that believes in you as a kid you will try to find the approval of other males for your self-esteem and I think a whole lot of gang membership or teen pregnancy or bizarre dating and anti-social behavior comes from people who never felt seen and loved by their fathers.

In fact the statistics I gathered from *Thefatherlessgeneration.com* on the damage to kids raised without an active father in their lives are pretty heart wrenching:

- 63% of youth suicides are from fatherless homes (US Dept. Of Health/Census) – 5 times the average.
- 90% of all homeless and runaway children

are from fatherless homes – 32 times the average.
- 85% of all children who show behavior disorders come from fatherless homes – 20 times the average. (Center for Disease Control)
- 80% of rapists with anger problems come from fatherless homes –14 times the average. (Justice & Behavior, Vol 14, p. 403-26)
- 71% of all high school dropouts come from fatherless homes – 9 times the average. (National Principals Association Report)
- 75% of all adolescent patients in chemical abuse centers come from fatherless homes – 10 times the average.
- 70% of youths in state-operated institutions come from fatherless homes – 9 times the average. (U.S. Dept. of Justice, Sept. 1988)
- 85% of all youths in prison come from fatherless homes – 20 times the average. (Fulton Co. Georgia, Texas Dept. of Correction)
- Daughters of single parents without a Father involved are 53% more likely to marry as teenagers, 711% more likely to have children as teenagers, 164% more

likely to have a pre-marital birth and 92% more likely to get divorced themselves.

So working out our marriage is a huge part of my need to provide for my kids.

This does NOT mean keeping our marriage together no matter what. After all - I don't want my kids to believe that they should ever be treated badly by anyone, and if they see me being mistreated by my husband that would be exactly what they would learn.

Keeping our marriage healthy involves plenty of fighting - not allowing us to take one another for granted. But it also means that we do fight to stay together and to do what is best for our family. It's always hard work - but hard work is necessary in everything in life. Fight for your marriage with all that you have - and fight with your husband to defend your beliefs and needs. That's how it goes. But giving your kids a good father who is a constant part of their lives is the greatest gift you can give them after being a good mother.

GOOD MOTHERS

Being a good mother?? Well, that means sacrifice. It means that you put yourself after your kids. For the rest of your life.

It means that you put your entire life on an alter and sacrificed it to the wellbeing of your children - and that your greatest hope for them is that they will someday do the same for their own children because once you have done so you realize that there is no greater joy than living your life for the sake of someone else. It's so true.

Also, don't buy the new agey crap that says that you need to get your "me-time" and take care of yourself first... etc. It's not that there isn't a lot of truth to it - there is, but this is spewed by women, like Oprah, who never raised kids. If you are a good mother there will be far more times than not that you will have to pick between "me-time" and what is best for your children and you HAVE to choose your children.

It all sounds pretty and nice to say that if you give yourself your 'me time' first that you will be a "better mom" and that you have to put the oxygen mask on yourself first being an important analogy for needing to put yourself first.

Well, it's crap. When you are doing your best as a mom you will have chipped nails and ponytail hair, and backaches that go un-massaged. But so did every other good mother since the beginning of time.

So what?

If you were running a marathon you wouldn't be pausing for some "me-time." If you took a break to get hydrated and rested (which of course would help you run better)- you would no longer be in the race. The truth is - once you're in the race there's not a lot of room for stopping and resting. It's hard - but that doesn't mean it's not worth it.

I would obviously acknowledge that we all, at times, need a break - but you take a break based on when it's best for your family. When can Dad take the kids for a bit? Do you have a good friend who you can trade an afternoon now and then? Can you shlep your well-behaved children with a box of chicken nuggets and get a pedicure? That's fine. It counts.

And remember these two things:

#1 Well behaved kids are worth their weight in gold. If you don't discipline your kiddos then you will need a whole lot more "me-time." Make the effort to teach your kids what behavior is and isn't allowed and everything will be so much easier. It takes work - it takes consistency. You have to decide that you will only ask your kids once and if they don't obey the very first time then they will be disciplined. Period. And you establish this when they are young.

It takes a few days of establishing the rules at home - then a few weeks of reinforcing that you will, in fact, punish them in the middle of Penny's in front of the whole world. (Because I promise, they can smell fear and will try to disobey you the minute they can tell that you would hate to deal with discipline in front of your girl-friends, who you just bumped into in the middle of the home goods section).

But once that kid KNOWS - doesn't think, or assume, but knows beyond a shadow of a doubt that you will make them horribly miserable if they don't obey you the first time, every time - then, and only then, will you have an obedient, polite child. And guess what? When your child is obedient and well behaved, you will enjoy being with them, and won't be nearly as desperate for 'me time.'

#2 It is over really, really, quickly. You feel like those sleepless nights in the first months will never end, and you just can't wait to sleep through the night. But then a couple of months later - they're over and you kinda miss it. The days of having a little one are short, soon they are in school and for most of the day you actually don't have to take care of them at all. And then they're in school all day and sports all evening and you really, really, don't see them except for dinner and breakfast. Then they're driving - then they're gone.

Instead of obsessing about "me-time" or your personal career goals - I would encourage you to focus on developing your relationship with your kids. Embrace your opportunities to teach them and cuddle them, and grow closer as a family. As a child of a close family I can tell you - you absolutely can remain in a close relationship with your parents after having grown if they invested in you and loved you. It keeps you bonded and you find that your parents are your best friends. On the other hand, if they grew up knowing your focus was on just surviving your time with them as though they were a chore - then their lives as adults will not include a friendship with you.

I'm not saying it isn't difficult. Motherhood is the most difficult, most self-sacrificing role I have ever had. But it is the most awesome. And if your relationship with your child is founded on respect and discipline and love, you will find that it goes much too fast, and you are going to embrace these kiddos and these years for the absolute treasure that they are. God's greatest blessing.

This is the final, ultimate lesson in the stages of pregnancy. It's time to completely totally change your world view.

THE MOST IMPORTANT LESSONS TO TEACH TO YOUR CHILDREN

There was a psychological study done in the 1970's on a group of 3-year-old children. A scientist would give them a marshmallow and tell them that they could eat it, but he was going to leave for five minutes, and if he came back and they hadn't eaten it, they could have two! Some managed to hold out and receive two marshmallows – other's shoved the first one in their mouths without a moment's hesitation.

The psychologist proceeded to track these children for decades. When the kids became adults there was a clear correlation between their ability to wait to eat the marshmallow and their success in life. That is because one of the most important indicators for success is our ability to exercise self-control.

When I was a girl my mother had a quote framed on the wall of our house. It said: "Failure is most often caused by giving up what we want most for what we want at the moment."

If you can teach your child to exercise self-control they will live a far more successful and happy life. They will have the ability to stick out education when they want to quit, to stick out marriages when they are attracted to a co-worker, to not succumb to massive debt or to unhealthy foods. The ability to want something in the moment, but control that desire in exchange for what you want long term cannot possibly be over-emphasized. If there is one lesson I think our rather hedonistic society has lost, it is the value and importance of self-control.

If you teach your children to simply obey, you really have not helped them become fully independent. Teaching them to control themselves, to make their choices with thought to the consequence - that is what creates a life of joy. But, as much as I think it is important to teach self-control there is one lesson that far supersedes – the most important lesson we can ever give our children: Kindness.

It is called the Golden rule, and from Jesus to Ghandi, Hinduism, Islam, Buddhism, Judaism, New Age-Wicca-Jain-Taosim with a touch of cinnamon, every worthwhile faith in the planet has a version of it.

"Do unto others as you would have done to you." Period.

Teach your children to be kind - to be kind to the

waitress, to their friends, and most of all to those who are weaker than them. A person who is focused on showing kindness to others is far less insecure. They aren't worried about what other's think of their clothes; they are too busy wondering how they can encourage someone else.

Kindness has a very messy nature. When spreading happiness we all just seem to get it on ourselves.

THE ULTIMATE LESSON OF MOTHERHOOD

IT'S NOT ABOUT YOU. IT NEVER WAS.

I know you thought that it was. I know your parents raised you to achieve great things. That you have been determined to follow your talents and rise to be all you can be. But you are going to discover the truth. That you have always been a link in a chain. Whether you had kids or not, your role is to do your best with the time you have and then to check out, having left the world a better place than you found it.

Now that you have kids you will begin to realize that a life of service to the next generation has begun. It's time to clean up other people's messes; to wipe rear ends, and boogers and vomit, and carry around an entire pharmacy in your bag.

You got a cute little diaper bag - I know - and you will have fun out with your cute stroller and bag having lunch with friends. Those days will be so fun. But you will also have days where you are throwing granola bars in a plastic grocery bag as you try to get out the door. And you know what? It's ok; you will begin to take pride in it.

As you surrender your desire for clean and tidy 'perfect' motherhood, you will let go of the Martha Stewart/Pottery Barn fantasy and you will embrace the little creature you made with all his little quirks and flaws.

You hated freckles on yourself, but you will adore them on your child. You always wished you were skinnier, but you realize how beautiful your daughter's round frame is. You always wanted curly hair, but think your son's fine straight hair is wonderful.

It is a chance to really love yourself by loving your children. It is beautiful and difficult. Miserable and wonderful.

Just like running a marathon or climbing a mountain, any great achievement requires difficult challenges. Meaning comes from the struggle. And lady you are going to struggle! Don't let anyone tell you otherwise.

But you are going to grow and love in ways you never ever knew. Welcome to the very coolest club in the world, Mom!

ACKNOWLEDGMENTS

Thank you to Kathy King and Harvey Rice I miss you both so much and love you forever. Your willingness to be creative, challenge ideas and try new things made me who I am.

Thanks to Ed Schwarzer for taking on a stranger and making her a daughter. I fight every day for parents to be determined by love - not blood because you proved which matters most.

Thanks to Krista Schwarzer for loving our crew as your own and bringing Shawn with you!

To Tyler, Trina and Stephen: Every memory and moment of our youth was blessed and I'm so grateful for all the dance parties in the kitchen with you three. I love you.

Chris Righter... my bestie... I'd never, ever have had the courage to try if not for you. Whatever life brings I love you and I'm so glad I'm on the journey with you.

Logan, Audrey, Rubyjane... I am so crazy, insanely in love with you. I hope you feel that love deep deep in your souls. My only real goal in life is to do this motherhood thing right. If I fail in every other way - I don't care, so long as I did this well.

Thank you to Mike Bray for giving me a chance - and a tequila sunrises - I am so grateful.

To Rachel, and all the editors and staff at City Lights and Wolf Pack Publishing, thanks for all your hard work.

To Matt Lindburg and Vincent Laboy thanks for believing in my voice even when it bucks tradition. I am so lucky you were brave with me.

To Tonya Maddox and Monica ... - thanks for your support.

To Rick LaPena - your notes are my favorite!

To Terri Leban I'm so grateful for a phone number on a slip of paper and your reputation... I owe you.

To Carlton Mason and the great people at CASA of the 7th - thank you for the chance to serve Foster kids and know that we really do make the world a better place.

Thank you Kirsten Miller for your advice... you have been a great friend I'm honored to raise our boys together

Trina Hobbs... Thanks for giving me the courage to dream big and ask.

Most importantly - thank you to Erika Story. Thanks for being my friend... Thanks for letting me write on your parenting blog. Thanks for hearing me out when I had a crazy idea and for suggesting pregnancy stories. Thanks for putting in hours of your life and emotional support behind a silly book and never giving me any guilt when I deserved so much. I owe you everything. Nothing I've ever written would exist without you.

Mr Dave Schelle - you once read a story of mine in class... it was huge for me. Doctor Flannery - when you read my paper on Machiavelli it made my year. Mrs. Hanson, Mr. Neil, Mr. Granell, Mr. Clay, Mrs. Chermak, Ma. and Pa Hayman, Pastor Harris, the chapel and theology dept of APU.

To Emily and Chris Cohick - you guys are the best!! To the Black Canyon Gymnastics mommies (and dad's) and coaches, and the people of Grace Community church... I'm so glad for your friendship.

To: Trina Hobbes, Amber Libbert, Kim and Chandra Cunningham, Darci Haueisen, Vanessa Hutton, Joanna Friesen, Denise and LaKeisha, Nita Smith, Stacey Young, Bethany Hall, Dena Lechner , Brandolynn Fillmore, and Emily Cohick. ❤❤❤ my list of besties... you are the soundtrack of my life.

ABOUT THE AUTHOR

For several years Twyla Righter has spent her time developing a specialized skill set. She can change a diaper on a squirming toddler – one handed. She can cook a dinner with an appropriate vegetable to carbohydrate/cheese ratio while quizzing a spelling test and refereeing a dramatic game of tag. She can teach a teenager to drive a manual and not completely lose her mind. These skills have yet to prove all that helpful to the world at large (but, the one handed diaper trick is a hit at parties.)

Twyla Righter lives in Colorado with a ridiculously sexy rock-climber and their three spawn.

www.ingramcontent.com/pod-product-compliance
Lightning Source LLC
LaVergne TN
LVHW041542070426
835507LV00011B/886